wishful thinking

wishful thinking

HOW I LOST MY FAITH
AND WHY I WANT TO FIND IT

Donna Freitas

New York Nashville

Worthy
Hachette Book Group
1290 Avenue of the Americas, New York, NY 10104
worthypublishing.com
twitter.com/worthypub

First edition: March 2024

Worthy is a division of Hachette Book Group, Inc. The Worthy name and logo are trademarks of Hachette Book Group, Inc.

The publisher is not responsible for websites (or their content) that are not owned by the publisher.

Worthy Books may be purchased in bulk for business, educational, or promotional use. For information, please contact your local bookseller or the Hachette Book Group Special Markets Department at special.markets@hbgusa.com.

Library of Congress Cataloging-in-Publication Data

Names: Freitas, Donna, author.
Title: Wishful thinking : how I lost my faith and why I want to find it
    / Donna Freitas.
Description: First edition. | New York, NY : Worthy/Hachette Book
    Group, 2024.
Identifiers: LCCN 2023040982 | ISBN 9781546004585 (hardcover) |
    ISBN 9781546004608 (ebook)
Subjects: LCSH: Faith. | Faith development. | Freitas, Donna—Religion. |
    Grief—Religious aspects—Christianity. | Psychological abuse—
    Religious aspects—Christianity. | Psychological abuse victims—
    Religious life.
Classification: LCC BV4637 .F7395 2024 | DDC 234/.23—dc23
    /eng/20231109
LC record available at https://lccn.loc.gov/2023040982

ISBNs: 9781546004585 (hardcover), 9781546004608 (ebook)
Printed in the United States of America
LSC-C
Printing 1, 2024

To my parents:
I like to imagine you are together again in the afterlife,
hanging out by some beautiful forever-ocean.
I hope you are. I miss you always.

Author's Note

Whenever I want to understand something really tricky, or if one of life's biggest questions is plaguing me, or if I am grieving or heartbroken or all of the above, I put whatever it is to my writing. I use the confines of a book and all the space it offers to try and come up with an answer, to get over the thing that has me hurting and lost, or to bring a little light back in if my days have grown particularly dark. Writing helps me to be in a mystery, and it functions a bit like a therapist's office at times—or as a confessional if the subject fits.

At the heart of this particular book is life's biggest riddle of all for me:

In a house like the one where I grew up, with parents like mine, with a mother who I've come to imagine as a kind of saint up in heaven—and as someone who went and got her doctorate in religious studies and theology—how in the world did I end up as a person without faith?

People talk about the mystery of faith. Well, for me it's pretty literal. Faith is an actual mystery, like in a novel where someone goes missing and we spend the next 300 pages trying to find out what happened, where they've gone, and if they're still alive or dead. I always tell my writing students to use the books they're working on to help solve something really important to them; that their book will take shape naturally if they write toward something they truly care about, even if that something is on the lighthearted side. Like, if you're working on a rom-com, make the love interest that guy you crushed on so hard in high school who never looked your way. In the novel version of that story, he falls madly in love with you! Or in the book inspired by your high school years, you get to vanquish the bully who made your life difficult and right the wrongs of the past. I mean, how good does that feel? Or best of all, you can conjure the people in your life you miss the most and experience them as alive again in the span of a couple hundred miraculous pages.

Books are miracles, they are grace, if we allow them to be.

I actually say that to people. I believe it's true. Reading books changes us, of course, stories open our minds and hearts and worlds. But writing them does, too—or it can, if we let ourselves be that open and vulnerable on the page. If we come to our books each day willing to lay our whole hearts out on the table, and bare our souls to ourselves. In my own life I've used the books I've written to do all sorts of important things—to ask for forgiveness, to engage in the conversations I missed out on with my mother when she was alive, to grieve painful losses, even to try and understand how I ended up an abuse victim at the hands of a Catholic priest. To ask, why did he pick me?

But throughout all my adult life, I've wanted to solve *my* mystery of faith. Why did I lose it? How did that happen? At what point did it go missing?

If I go back to the scene of the crime and go over all of my steps carefully enough, where I've been, *exactly*, first as a child, then as a teenager and college student, and eventually as a grad student and married person, will I be able to pinpoint the source of the disappearance and follow the trail of clues? If I interview enough witnesses on the page, and identify the relevant evidence over the course of my life that led me to the place I am now, still searching for what happened, will I finally figure it out? Will my faith be waiting there for me, after all this time?

I honestly don't know. And because of this, I've always been afraid to put this mystery to a book. What if I finally let myself try and solve it, only to find out I'm too late? That what I'm searching for is over and done with and gone forever? Like a cold case that plagues a detective, but one who worries if she finally solves the crime, it will only lead to more pain for everyone involved? A kind of hollowness at the end of the road?

But now here I am, after so much resistance, and after trying to put this mystery to bed for a few decades without having solved it. I'm going to do what I always have and write toward an answer because I can't seem to turn away from this file in the storage room of my brain. I don't have to imagine my faith has gone missing like in a novel, either, because it's been absent for decades in my very real life. And even though I'm a little afraid because the stakes couldn't be higher and I'm not sure what I'm writing toward, I'm going to put my detective hat back on in this effort to find my answer once and for all: At the end of this road, will I find a faith with a still-beating heart, however faint, or something long gone and impossible to resuscitate?

Part I
Precocious Atheist

1

I discover I'm alone.

The sun is out. I am six. It's after school and I'm sitting cross-legged on my mother's flowered bedspread, the same one she had for most of my childhood. It's maroon and made of a sturdy, rough-feeling cotton, with swirls of blue and white flowers, laced with a mustard color, the green of stems and branches. The light filters through the windows on two sides of the room.

My mother is folding laundry.

I can see her moving in the long, horizontal mirror on the wall above the chest of drawers where she keeps her sweaters, socks, T-shirts. Jewelry boxes and little trays with earrings and necklaces are arranged neatly on top of it. She has short curly hair, a soft bosomy body. A smile on her face as she talks to me. I watch as she picks up one thing after the other from a giant mountain of clothing on the bed, white undershirts that my father wears each day, his boxer shorts, her nightgowns, my pajamas. She keeps reaching for the pile, plucking a garment from it, holding the piece of clothing up in the light to begin folding it, bending down to press it smooth against the bedspread, to make clear creases along the fabric. Then she stacks her finished work to the side. The cycle continues. The pile diminishes and the neatly folded stacks grow taller.

We talk. About my day at school. About life. We do this all the time. Me sitting on my mother's bed, keeping her company while she folds.

I ask her questions. A lot.

It's a joke between her and my father, how many questions I have, how I can't help asking things constantly, how my questions usually aren't of the easy variety. Not the *When are we going to leave?* kind, or even the *What makes thunder happen?* ones that have straight-forward, scientific explanations. I ask those, too. I always want to know *when* this, and *how* that. But my questions are more often the sort that don't have an obvious answer. *How do you know when you go to bed at night that another day will be there when you wake up? Why do people die? Why do I exist? Why do you exist?*

The question on the docket for my mother today is one of the biggest of all: about the nature of God. It swirls in my little brain as she folds and talks, and I get ready to lay it down between us, trying to find the right words to begin.

I remember, vividly, another conversation I had with my dad about the mind and thoughts and what it means to be a person. It's one of those memories that's lasted a lifetime, that's come back to me again and again over the years, one that has formed me. One that began to form me the moment it happened.

"I am always having thoughts," I told my father one Saturday morning. He and I were sitting on the living room floor, on one of those oval braided rugs my parents had all over the house. The television was on and playing cartoons, though my father and I weren't paying attention. My Legos were out, and we were building.

"Thoughts go through my head constantly, one after the other, when I'm awake. It's like a voice inside my brain. Are you always having thoughts?" I asked him. "Do you have a voice inside your head that's talking?"

"Yes," my father answered. He seemed mountainous next to me, but the gentlest of mountains. "Our minds are always working and going. Even when we are asleep."

"Can you hear *my* thoughts?"

I remember my dad stopping to look at me, putting down the Lego block in his hand. "No, I can't hear what's happening in your mind, sweetheart. No one can."

"I can't hear what's happening in anyone else's head," I said, as though this was up for debate. "Only in mine."

"Yes, that's right."

"Why can't we hear each other's thoughts?"

My father seemed to consider this. The light of the television shifted next to us, and shifted again, the swirl of cartoons constantly moving across the screen. The rug was littered with the primary colors of the plastic blocks. My father was a kind man, willing to listen to me no matter what, fielding my million questions with a patience that seemed endless. This willingness never waned, not as long as he was alive. "Well, we just can't, sweetheart," he said. "We're not made that way."

"But why? Why aren't we made that way?"

"I don't know," my father said.

I remember pausing to calculate what all of this meant. I've always been someone who does the math, who goes from one idea to the next to try and figure out how everything adds up, to gain some understanding, conclude as much as I can from the information on hand. When I was ready to speak again, I said, "But that means you can never hear the voice in my head and my thoughts, and I can never hear the voice in your head and your thoughts. I can never be in someone else's head to hear what they're thinking. And no one can ever be in my head to hear what I'm thinking."

"That is what it means, sweetheart, yes," he confirmed.

"But doesn't that also mean we're all alone?"

My father watched me. For a while, he was silent.

I waited. I wanted him to tell me otherwise, that my conclusions were wrong. I didn't want to be alone in my thoughts, alone in my head, for an entire lifetime. This idea was unbearable. I wanted to learn the method of reaching inside the mind of someone else to hear their constant stream of consciousness, I wanted to hand them the key to my own brain so they could do the same. I worried if I could never find a way to do this that some cataclysmic level of loneliness would always be mine. I wanted connection, not isolation. I wanted it even as a little girl.

What I wanted was God. At its root, that's what this conversation with my father was about. I know this now, even if I couldn't name it back then.

"In a way, it does mean we're alone," my father said eventually, and oh so carefully. "But you can tell me your thoughts, sweetheart, and I can tell you mine. That's why we talk to each other like this. That's why we have conversations. So we can share our thoughts and feelings. So we can connect and so we aren't alone."

I nodded. *Yes.* But then I shook my head. *No.*

"It still makes me feel alone," I told him. "I think it's strange I can never hear what's in anyone's head and they can never hear what's in mine."

I find it strange even now, decades later. I am in awe of this fact of our being. I both love and also hate it.

This awe of mine, this simultaneous love and hatred for how we are constructed as humans, and my awareness about this natural state of isolation, took me down a path that turned me into a philosophy major and eventually a PhD. I was built with a fundamental desire to be known and to know others, and this desire seemed constantly active in my DNA. I wanted a work-around for this stumbling block and I would soon begin searching for it everywhere. I wanted to tear down the walls between our minds, most of all my own, to make my brain porous, open, available.

I think what I've always wanted is to let God in.

"I suppose it is strange, sweetheart," my father agreed.

We went back to our Legos.

"Did you know there were other gods?" There I am on the bed again, with my mother folding laundry. My burning question finally out in the open.

My mother holds up one of my father's undershirts, folds the short white sleeves inward and presses it to the bed, then looks at me. "What do you mean?"

I explain what happened in school that day. We were doing our phonics lesson, sounding out words and sentences and entire short excerpts of texts. As my classmates were struggling to articulate each syllable on the page, I was focused elsewhere, mind racing. I began to grasp not only the words we were uttering out loud, but also their meaning. Short excerpts about Greek gods. Apollo. Athena. Zeus and the gang. My six-year-old brain short-circuited.

"You never told me there were other gods," I say to my mother. "I thought there was only one god."

My mother keeps folding, thinking about how to answer my accusation.

Because it *is* an accusation. I feel tricked.

"There are lots of stories about other gods," she says. "There are lots of religions, sweetheart. But we believe in the Catholic God."

"But why *this* God and not one of the others?"

"Because we believe that this is the true God."

"But how do you *know*?"

"Because we have faith."

I am doing the math in my head again and it is not adding up the way I want it to. "But what if we picked the wrong God? What if one of the *other* gods is the real God? How can we know if we're right?"

My mother stops folding to look at me. "Sweetheart, we can't. That's what faith is. Faith is believing in your heart that something is right and true even if you can't know for sure. Not in a way you can see or touch. You just have to believe it."

Here's something you need to understand about my mother:

She was a champion believer. Like, an Olympic one. My grandmother was more of a believer of convenience. Everyone else was doing it, so she did it, too. Grandma would get all gussied up, stuff her pocketbook with money for the collection basket, a packet of tissues, and her rosary, preferably a nice sparkly one, and trot off to mass on Sundays. Grandma did love her saints, and I loved the opulent way in which she loved them. Baby Jesus under a great dome of glass. Framed, golden portraits of saints. But my mother was the real deal. She glowed with belief, and it surrounded her like a halo.

As I sit there on my parents' bed, staring up at this Olympic gold medalist in the sport of faith, I consider my mother's lobbying for my own belief, but it's just not adding up in my head.

"That doesn't make sense," I tell her. Because I cannot make sense of what she is telling me. I am staring at the floral comforter, eyes blurring, my little young heart pounding. I am really and truly traumatized by this news, by this entire day, by the knowledge it has brought. "I'm worried that we picked the wrong God," I go on, distraught. I look up at my mother, see the expression on her face, the curiosity in her eyes as she looks down at me, her daughter. The shadows there, the concern, but also the love. "Aren't you worried, too?" I ask her.

"No, sweetheart," she says, surely, calmly, gently, much like my father. Then she breaks our stare, reaches for the top of the laundry pile again. "Because I have faith."

I speak of that Legos conversation with my father as one of the memories that formed me—one of the memories that continues to form me. But that afternoon with my mother is, I think, the primary memory that made me who I am in terms of faith. The conversation that began my journey of faith formation, or maybe it's better said, *de*formation. I don't like that word applied to myself, but perhaps it is the truth and I need to own it. Or perhaps it's something else and my task is to discover what. Regardless, that discussion about other gods and which God is the right God is the beginning of everything with faith and me. I know this in my gut, my heart, my brain, my soul.

But the beginning of what, exactly? A loss of faith? A planting of the seeds of so much doubt? A lifetime of it?

Sometimes I'm able to look at that faith talk with my mother another way, wonder if maybe instead of a loss, it is a gain. Instead of it beginning to *unmake* my faith, sending it awry, it started me on a path of my very own. That I should see it as the opening of a life-long journey that will have me continually questioning what faith is, who God is, what it means to be a believer. People go entire lifetimes without ever thinking about their faith—I know this. They just have it without worry or complication, theirs to enjoy. (Or perhaps, theirs to ignore?) But not me. I don't get to enjoy faith. I get to search for it. Wish for it. Long for it with every breath. Every single day of my existence.

Whereas people like my mother take leaps of faith like Olympian long jumpers, I am also an Olympian of sorts, yet not the good kind.

I'm more like the athlete who keeps crumbling under pressure, walking right up to the edge of the high dive and choking, turning around and walking back, climbing down the ladder to the ground. All my life, I've gone back and forth, back and forth on the diving board of faith, standing there in my ugly swimsuit and bathing cap, funny goggles on my face, curling my bare toes over the edge of the rough, narrow plank, swinging my arms, trying to prepare myself to jump, then looking down. Seeing only cement. So I step away, retreat completely, until I find the courage to climb up the ladder again, walk out to the edge, and look down once more, hoping maybe this time I will see the water; that maybe this time I'll find the courage to jump.

Maybe all this doubt of mine is God's way of talking to me. Maybe God has been having a conversation with me ever since the day I opened my phonics book and began to read about Greek gods. I want it to be this. I want it to be God's way of reaching for me. Through the voice, the words, the conversations I had with my mother while she was alive, with my father, too, and my most cherished teachers, and so many wonderful friends. On my best days, it is this notion that shines through all of my darkness, like sunlight.

That afternoon with my mother explaining to me about faith was the start of a back-and-forth between us about God, religion, my atheism, that continued as I grew up, as I left the house for college and eventually went to grad school. My atheism, like a possession, an affliction. My mother wanted faith for me while she was alive, more than anything. She'd throw it toward me like a lifeline because it was a lifeline for her, tossing it outward like she was on a boat and I was in the sea, drowning, even though I'd just sit there, treading water in the darkness and the swells. I always refused to take what she offered, refusing to swim toward the rope. She kept trying to reach me with it anyway. She never stopped. Then she died. More than twenty years ago.

Even after my mother's death, I still talk to her about faith, God, all she believed. Because she gave me this, too, this notion that it is perfectly normal to talk to the dead. She did it all the time so why shouldn't I? She talked to the saints, she talked to the people of her childhood, long gone. So now I tilt my head toward the sky and imagine her up there in all that blue. I conjure her in my head while I'm cooking in the kitchen, hear her voice giving me directions. Because I know my mother was right about this. She was right to keep trying to convince me what faith could offer a person, and sharing what it offered her during her time on this earth.

I want that lifeline, too.

2
Angels in the backseat.

The world is dark. Snow is thick on the ground. It's a few days before Christmas and I am in graduate school. The phone rings in my apartment and I reach for it.

"Your father was in an accident," my mother says when I pick up.

My entire body tingles with cold, fear, panic. "Is he okay?" I ask, even though I can tell from her voice that he is not.

"He's in the hospital. You need to come home."

The sky outside my windows is black, the light in my apartment is gray and shadowy. I get up and start flipping switches, turning on lamps, trying to chase away the dread and the darkness. "What aren't you saying, Mom? Tell me, please?"

"Just get in the car, sweetheart," she says, sounding exhausted. In a little under a year, she will be diagnosed with late-stage ovarian cancer, but we don't know this yet. "Drive safely."

I hang up.

My heart is pounding, my blood is racing.

I gather my things, get dressed, grab my keys, and go.

I've always loved my father. He was a beautiful person. Lonely and proud, in a way that makes my heart ache. Smart and kind and generous. Also, very funny, but with a subtle kind of humor.

He could be stubborn, though, and reckless. In ways that nearly killed him, killed my mother, killed me. He was prone to depression his whole life. When he was depressed, he did not take care of himself, and this affected others, especially us, his family. An existential despair swam within him, deep and endless. It cut him to his soul.

I am so much my mother, but I am also so much him. If I had to guess, my own propensity for darkness, my acute sense of the abyss, came from my father. If this propensity is something in my biological makeup, then he was the parent who passed it along. I don't begrudge him this. However painful this darkness is inside me, this loneliness so deep and gaping that it sometimes frightens me, it's also intrinsically tied to the best parts of who I am. When I'm in that darkness, really in it, this is when I most long for God to find me, to show me that God's there. This darkness both keeps God from me and opens me to God. I know this to my soul.

When over the course of my life I saw my father struggling with the darkness that was his, it scared me. I know how deep it goes. I know how I feel when I am in it. I worried it would take my father from me, because it almost took him in the past, multiple times, from both of us when my mother was still alive. So I learned to watch for it within him, to search for its appearance, became acutely aware it might awaken at any moment. For the whole of my adult life, I trained myself to be there for my father to catch it, to try and prevent it from taking him from this earth.

Lucky for me, I have my writing and my pursuit of philosophy, the means I use for dragging myself out of the abyss and toward the light again, but my father never had these tools. He didn't have books and creative outlets or even a college degree. He was the man at the bar, the one you see there every day, sitting alone, the working-class man who lives a hard life who might say hello to the people nearby and certainly to the bartender who knows him, but who mainly just sits on the barstool, quiet, in his thoughts. Alone with the voice in his head, the one I could never hear. What was that voice saying while my father drank his martini each night? I wish I could go back and access it, I wish I could have taken some of my father's darkness away, or at least to have been there in it with him. Prove to him we were always in this together, he and I. Even if we were unable to heal each other's darkness, as we both lived it side by side.

Then again, maybe he knew I was like him in this way. Maybe we did live side by side in this darkness we shared, even if we didn't say it out loud. Maybe, maybe.

"The angels saved your father!" My mother says this the second she comes through the door from the garage. She's just been to the lot where the car was towed after my father's accident, to see the damage, to retrieve his things.

The sun is out again. I am in the kitchen of the house where I grew up, standing in front of the long butcher block island at its center. A big sliding glass door is behind me, along with a set of windows above the sink, and the glare from the snow on the ground outside is bright against my mother's tearstained face. I've been pacing the kitchen, waiting for her to come home, and stressed about my dad.

"What do you mean?" I ask my mother.

There is no Christmas in our house this year, no New Year's. My father is lying in a hospital bed, lucky to be alive. He survived a head-on collision on his way home late the other night. The other woman was okay, but he was not. The accident was his fault, at least this is what I glean from my mother over the course of several days, but she never tells me this directly, we never discuss what's going on with my father openly. This is how we are in my family, even though this accident comes after a series of other horrible tragedies, losses, all related to him. One after the other they befall us, and we break a little more each time, but we talk around them rather than about them. In the very near future, when my mother is diagnosed with cancer, my father will blame himself. He will believe my mother's cancer is on account of these terrible years we lived because of his struggles, and this will bring about more pain and suffering that we do not discuss directly.

But right now, my mother is on the other side of the butcher block island, keys still gripped in her hand, bulky winter coat bundled around her body even though it's warm in here from all that sun.

"Your father had angels in the backseat of his car," she says, like this should tell me all I need to know. "*My* angels."

And in a way, it does.

My mother loved angels. She put them all over the house.

Big ones, small ones, felt ones, papier-mâché ones, ceramic angels, glass figurine angels that caught the sunlight, refracted it, sending rainbows all over the walls, the furniture. We made angels in the snow when I was little, and my mother made them with her nursery school students on all kinds of occasions. She always found reasons to be conjuring angels with construction paper and glue, with pipe cleaners, crayons and paints and markers. She would bring tiny statue angels home from the store. My mother believed in angels like she believed in the saints. She populated our lives with both. Saints and angels. They would dangle in a mobile in front of the windows or from the rearview mirror of the car. It was a normal part of my childhood to see them all around us.

But on Christmas? The angels really came out in our house.

I had favorites as a child. There were angels with long flowing hair that I thought were so beautiful, I would sit and stare at them, and wish I looked just like them. There were felt ones about two feet tall that she'd set by the door, their mouths open in song, wings wide and flying.

Our nativity scene was replete with them. Each year, after the Thanksgiving leftovers were put away in the fridge, I was allowed to set up our manger in the living room, right next to the place where we would put up the Christmas tree. Our family nativity scene had all the necessities: Joseph, Mary, Baby Jesus, the Wise Men, a whole bunch of animals. Lots of sheep, little lambs. There was a stable where everyone could hang out and some fake hay to scatter around. But along with our nativity we set up a giant chorus of angels. I'm talking two dozen little angel figurines, dressed in pink robes, lilac ones, pale-blue ones. I'm not even sure whose idea it was to have so many angels flanking Joseph and Mary and the Three Wise Men. The angels did not come with the nativity set. This was a Freitas family addition.

I would arrange and rearrange those angels. Like, on a daily basis. Sometimes in a V-formation, like birds flying south. Sometimes in a half circle. Sometimes I'd scatter them all over, as though they were a NYC holiday crowd waiting outside *The Today Show* windows, looking in on Baby Jesus. Sometimes I'd move them around hourly, unable to decide where they were best positioned. It was a Christmastime hobby of mine.

My mother dressed me up as an angel for school once when I was little. It must have been for some kind of Christmas pageant. There are photos of me, mouth open and singing in a white dress, with wings and a gold pipe cleaner halo. And how I loved that these beautiful winged beings were all over our house, in my room and Grandma's, too, that they could be called up on a snow day with our bodies.

"They watch over us," my mother always said. "They keep us safe."

I enjoyed this idea for as long as it lasted.

For as long as I managed to believe it could be true.

My mother is still in her coat and holding her keys, talking to me over the kitchen island.

"The angels I made for the teachers at school," she is explaining. "They were in the backseat of your father's car."

My mother was creative with construction paper and other, similar tools of the nursery school teacher. Every year she would make cookies for everyone we knew on Christmas, and she'd make cookies and angels for her colleagues. She wanted angels for everybody. She'd cut out circles, halve them, take the half circle and staple it into a cone to make the angel's body. Then she would attach wings to each side, another circle for the head, add halos, simple faces. They were delicate and lovely and very my mother. Like everything she made by hand, they would take forever to complete and sometimes she would rope us into helping her, conscript us into a kitchen table assembly line with scissors and paper and glue.

"The angels are why your father survived," she says to me now.

I still don't quite understand. "What are you talking about, Mom?"

She goes on to explain how, in her effort to get ready for school the last day before the Christmas holidays—which was also the day of my father's accident—she put her homemade angels into the car that afternoon so she wouldn't forget them the next morning. She had so many things she needed to bring for the various school celebrations and gift giving, she'd prepared ahead. Then my father took the car that night, with the angels sitting there, watching over him in the backseat.

"That's why he's still alive," she said.

I nod. I don't actually believe this, but I know enough not to say this to my mother.

She tells me that when she finally found the car in the tow lot, she threw up next to it onto the snow because she couldn't believe my father survived a crash that resulted in so much damage. The crush of the metal was shocking to see, she says. The entire front of the car was destroyed all the way to the driver's seat. And yet, sitting there, right behind my father, were the three dozen construction paper angels, their delicate wings out, halos floating over their heads. They hadn't even fallen to the floor or tipped over at all.

Tears are running down her face as she tells me this story. "They were so perfect, Donna. Somehow they didn't move during the accident. There were rows of them standing up in the backseat, untouched by the force of it. I know that's why your father lived."

I stand there, trying to think of how to respond. Unlike me, my mother sees evidence of God everywhere she turns. Belief is natural, as easy as breathing. This awe of God's presence is so alive in my mother that her faith is always bubbling up in conversation, in the prayers she utters out loud while she is cooking or moving around the house, even while she is driving, and in the projects she makes with her kids at school. How can it be that I am the daughter of such a believer? Why is it my father could pass on his capacity for existential despair, but I failed to receive my mother's capacity to experience God in every molecule of life, in all of existence, even in a family tragedy, like my father's accident?

"The angels watched over him," she insists.

Her voice is full of awe. Faith. Belief. Gratitude. To the angels, to God.

I want to feel this, too. I want to believe it. The truth is, I don't. But I believe in my mother. I have faith in her. Totally and completely. This, at least, is a start.

3

I want to believe.

Many years later, long after my father's accident and decades beyond that afternoon with my mother when my struggle with God was born, my husband left me. One morning, he woke up and within forty-five minutes he had packed a bag and walked out the door, never to return.

I broke.

It wasn't the first time I'd been broken. But it might be one of the worst ones. I couldn't sleep, I lost my appetite. My friends came over to babysit me. Day and night, night and day. I fantasized about walking into traffic, falling from the roof of my building. I lost the will to live. I wept and sobbed and wept some more. Often on the wood floor of my living room. As I lay there, I wondered:

God, where are you?

If you're really out there, now is the time to show yourself.

I need you.

Please.

I thought of my mother while I cried. I think of my mother often in general, but I especially thought of her then. How much I needed her. How much I wanted her to get on a train like she used to when she was alive and I was going through something difficult, and come down to see me wherever I was living at the time. She would show up at my apartment, roller bag and all, and start to clean everything. If I was low on supplies, she'd go out and buy them, then begin scrubbing and Windexing and dusting and organizing. Next would be the supermarket trip for groceries. Afterward she would cook a sauce, make meatballs, feed me. Make sure to stuff my fridge with food before she left.

During those months after my husband walked out, I wished for God, I wished for my mother, I wished for God again. I thought of my mother's relationship with God. I remembered the "Footprints" poem on its little wooden stand in her bedroom. The card was laminated, the words on one side of it, the footprints in the sand winding their way up the other. I would read and reread it as a child while I sat on the rug or her bed, watching TV. I would sometimes stand up and stare at it closely, pondering those footprints and what the poem meant.

So as I lay on the floor of my now-empty apartment, empty of my husband, empty of hope, empty of all but me, an adult woman left and alone, I thought of those footprints. I wished for the poem to be true. I wished for the experience of being carried because I could no longer walk on my own. I was too broken to stand, to take a step by myself. This was supposed to be the time it would happen. If there was a moment I needed faith, when I needed God, this was it.

I waited and waited.

I waited to be lifted up off that floor and held and carried by God. *Please. Please, God. I need you. Help me.*

I have always wanted God.

I've set this book up as a mystery of faith, and God is at the heart of this mystery, this want of mine that never goes away. Even as I've rejected God, brushed off my hands and muttered, "I'm done with you, dude," underneath all that rejection is desire. Lingering, unwavering, simmering below my denial. Like some kind of boyfriend you can't make yourself get over, one you tell your friends you're done with but inside you know you're lying.

My want has taken different shapes over the years. At times, it has been stronger, more visible than at others, but it is always with me, like a secret born inside my heart that will never leave no matter how many times I try to dispel it. It is an ache, a longing, vast and unyielding. As real to me as my hands and feet.

The problem is that while the ache is unmistakable, God is not.

So I long and I wish and I wait.

And I try to solve for God.

I may have lost my faith as a child, misplaced it very young. But I have never stopped searching to find it again because if my mother taught me anything, she instilled the notion that our belief in God is precious. Like life or death and nothing less. The sun, the moon, all creatures great and small, the lives we live, and the deaths beyond them.

My mother tried so hard to hand me this key that would unlock something in the universe, in every living, breathing thing among us, inside of me, something beyond death and grief. She knew the years ahead would bring unimaginable loss, losses beyond herself and my father, losses she could not possibly anticipate, that this was as inevitable for her daughter as it is for all of us, as it was for her. Losses like the one that became the end of my first marriage. She would not be there forever, so she was offering me all she could while she was still alive, the means to help me move beyond these future tragedies.

Within Christianity, within the resurrection, my mother found a way through, a way to hang on despite the grief of being alive. This is the story Christianity offers, isn't it? A way through the devastation that is a single human life, to something more. A way beyond death to something like joy, a willingness to endure, a truth that while there is loss, there is also always love and this love is much bigger than all the deaths in human history. I can still feel my mother from beyond the grave, trying to offer me this one, sustaining thing. The key pressed to the floor underneath her toe, she is trying to scoot it across to me. I love her for this. I always will.

Precocious atheist.

I don't remember who first applied this term to me, but once I heard it, I couldn't unhear it. The label was sticky. It attached to me and never let go. It happened during college at Georgetown. During one of my classes I told the story of how a first-grade phonics lesson shattered my six-year-old world and then my relationship to faith was never the same. Class ended, someone came up to me and said, "You're one of those precocious atheists."

This term swirled in the air above my head and I breathed it into my nose like a poisonous gas. I parsed it in my head. Precocious, i.e., advanced. Plus, atheist. Nonbeliever. *Un*believer. Precocious atheist equals a person who loses her faith early in life, even as a child. Yes, I thought. That's right in my case. I did have faith before that phonics lesson. There is a before and after from that moment which is a flash memory in my brain. Then the sunlight coming through the windows following school, and my mother reflected in the mirror above the chest of drawers and her jewelry boxes.

I've been trying to find the antidote ever since this term was applied to me. *Precocious* usually means something positive, but in this case, I don't agree. I'm not sure being advanced at atheism is good for a young child. I'm not sure anyone should aspire to excel at an early age toward the existential anxiety that inevitably accompanies a loss of faith, an entire life without it. The label has been like a tar over the years, dark and viscous, a relentless stain on my person.

I want it off.

There is another question about this label that grows louder as I get older, and haunts me: What if I'd never heard this stupid term? What if that person after my class never named it as mine? What if I hadn't allowed it to seep into me? Sometimes I think this label stole something from me, took it, mercilessly. It entered my path at a significant juncture, while I was searching for Meaning during college, when really what I wanted was God. During childhood and young adulthood, I zigzagged constantly between something like faith and something like atheism. I had a surplus of doubt, an excessive amount of it. But back then, I still could have been saved.

I often wish I could return to that moment and that person with their stupid label so I could tell them to get it and themselves away from me. Because I want to swim in faith, bathe in it, walk in it. I wanted it then and I want it now. To have it and hold it until death do us part. I search for it. I *desire* it. With my whole heart and with all that I am.

So there I am, lying on the floor, my husband gone, alone and weeping. Broken in a way that feels beyond repair. Waiting for God. Still. Like Simone Weil, and her book of the same name.

But I am about to give up.

On God. Who, as usual, is not showing up.

All I can see is the abyss. A bottomless pit of darkness, loneliness, emptiness. This is the truth that swallows me. No one is coming. No one is going to pick me up off this floor. It is going to be me who does it or I'll be on this floor forever. The "Footprints" poem is wishful thinking and nothing more. It may apply to other people, but not to me.

In the moments of my deepest grief, when all is lost or seems that way, I become acutely aware of this other grief that is a wide and gaping wound within me. When I am peering into the abyss, into that bottomless pit of nothingness that my philosophy major at Georgetown first helped me to name, I can see this wound so clearly. It will stare back at me through the darkness and the tears and most of all through the loneliness. A particular grief piled onto all that other grief.

A particular kind of *grieving*.

The absence of God. A lack of faith, the impossibility of God finding me, of me finding God, the truth of this. God and I are like some story of a missed connection. We are always poised to meet each other, always on the verge of running into each other on the very same block in a city of millions, yet somehow our meeting never occurs. We are meant to be, yet tragically we're never able to find each other. Why can't we just manage to be together for once? Why can't we just have our happy ending? Otherwise, to be me is to live in a constant state of faith-induced grief, a never-ending wave of loss, an emptiness that never quite leaves. I can feel the loss there, this gaping absence, its fingers reaching for me, even on my best days.

Maybe this is simply classic Dark Night of the Soul stuff. Where God is actually with me even if I can't feel God there. So I wander the wilderness, waiting to be found.

Because it is also true that during the rest of my life, say, when I am not recently left by my husband and sobbing on the floor of my living room, during the times when the world feels full, when the abyss recedes far enough that I can nearly forget it's there, I wonder if this faith I wish for is staring me right in the face and I just miss it. Like, something is wrong with my vision so I'm unable to see God looking straight into my eyes, the very God for whom I keep searching. God is standing in front of me near the corner deli where I live in Brooklyn, and God is speaking, saying out loud, "Donna Freitas, I am right here with you. I am. See me."

4
Sick Soul seeks salvation.

William James describes three kinds of believers. The healthy-minded, the divided selves, and the sick souls.

I first read his *Varieties of Religious Experience* in graduate school, searching for understanding, trying to diagnose myself and all the people around me, too. I envied the healthy-minded. The people for whom faith comes easily, for whom it is their most natural state of being. For them, faith is a boon, a joy, a comfort and a companion across the span of life.

But I am either a divided self at best, or at worst, one of those sick souls James describes. I can never decide which. Maybe I am a little of both.

For James, St. Augustine was the classic divided self. Tortured, wayward. Full of doubt. Agonizing constantly over his every action, his every thought, wondering if it drew him closer or farther away from God, worrying that every tiny digression turned him into a sinner, even his cries as a baby. I often want to label St. Augustine a sick soul, but what defines him as a divided self for James is what Augustine believed and knew: he was meant to live a life marked by faith and commitment to God and the good, as opposed to a life of sin. The divided self knows how to make itself whole even if it struggles to achieve this, even if it struggles against getting there. And even though St. Augustine struggled mightily with his desires (*Oh, Lord, make me chaste, just not yet!*), he knew exactly where to go, exactly how to resolve the divide within to make himself whole again. And eventually, he did just that.

Case closed. More or less. Or so the story goes.

But the sick soul is prone to despair. That person with a close and personal relationship with the abyss, existential angst, the person who sounds a lot like me. As with the divided self, there is an upside to the sick soul. She is a candidate to be born again. A person whose resolution and healing of this sickness involves a vivid and whole transformation of self; who, if she can just see beyond the abyss, might find in herself an openness to falling or, better said, *leaping*, straight into the darkness without fear. A person who digs through the emptiness and finds within herself a willingness to participate in the ultimate of trust falls, once again climbing up to that high dive of faith, rung by rung, funny goggles on her face. She'll walk straight to the end of the diving board and, without looking back, this time she'll finally find the courage to jump.

Part II
The Jesus Years

5

If you pray for it, it will come.

The house where I grow up is a ranch house, one story, painted white. It has red-wine-colored shutters around the windows, a long front porch. My mother is always out in the yard, gardening gloves on, weeding, planting, clipping, unafraid of the worms and bugs that wiggle their way to the surface of the soil as she cultivates it. The worms, she tells me, are a sign of the soil's health. Evidence of God's meticulous handiwork.

When my family settles in Narragansett, Rhode Island, one of the things my mother is most excited about is the yard she will get to plant and water and dot with tulips, perennials, one beautiful cherry tree, and a young birch, her favorite. Her gardening tools are always nearby, her knees set on the scratchy brown rug she inches along as she works her way across the many flower beds. This is how our neighbors meet my mother. They walk by and raise their hands in a wave or make their way across the new grass to greet her; they talk about how lovely it is to see this person next door working hard to beautify her lawn. My mother's green thumb seems to have turned the rest of her fingers that same lush hue upon our arrival, because soon there is color everywhere, hanging from the flowerpots on the porch, in the back by my swing set, outside the windows of my room. My mother and that other mother, Nature, are longtime friends.

My mother loves to garden so much that later in life, when she is dying of cancer and too weak to make the annual spring pilgrimage to the garden center to pick out flowers for the beds meandering through our yard, my father does something I will never forget—my father who, like me, was not born with a green thumb or anything resembling one. He carefully packs my mother into the car, brings her to pick out all the flowers she wants—pansies, marigolds, daisies—then carts her home and sets up one of the kitchen chairs on the lawn so his dying wife can sit. Then my father kneels down on her gardening rug, tools set up next to him, and takes direction from her about what's a weed to pull and what's not, where to plant this flower and that bulb. He does this day after day, brings out the chair for my mother to sit, kneels down on that rug, digs, plants, turns the soil under her watchful gaze. He wears a large pair of gardening gloves purchased for this purpose, my mother's too small for his hands. He works in his wife's gardens until she is too tired to sit any longer, until she is satisfied the gardens have been sufficiently cultivated for the time being.

My mother's happy places are: the garden, the beach, the kitchen, the Catholic school where she teaches, and the Catholic church where we attend mass. So they are all of ours, too.

Now picture this: my grandmother's bedroom. Flowered wallpaper, a perfectly made bed, an ironing board always ready to go, a small, box television set up in front of it, the twin to the one in my parents' room. Grandma is a champion ironer and she is constantly asking me for stuff to iron after she retires. She irons while she watches her soaps: *Days of Our Lives, One Life to Live, General Hospital.* Before this, Grandma was the first woman manager at Raytheon, but that is a story for another time.

When my family and I move into our ranch house in Rhode Island, to my delight Grandma has moved with us, taking up residence at the far end of the house a few short steps from my bedroom. I take full advantage of her proximity, constantly visiting her, asking questions, keeping her company during her soaps, and best of all, partaking of the many treasures around her room.

A long dresser lines one entire wall with an equally long, tall mirror above it. A lace doily runner brought over from Italy decorates the dresser. Spread out neatly on top of it are my grandmother's jewelry boxes. Grandma loves her jewelry. She'll wear her rings and necklaces and earrings to go out to Stop & Shop to buy bananas and milk. She's an old-school Italian lady in this way. I have black-and-white photos of her dressed in a faux-fur-collared coat as she works the register at her family's Italian market as a teenager, dark lipstick stark against her skin, earrings dangling. She has always loved her glamour.

She and I are besties.

Grandma is the person who imparts to me her love of shopping, fashion, and all things shiny. She will drive me to school in her enormous white Lincoln Town Car with its red leather top, and teaches me to love Woolworths and its vast array of cheap nail polish and makeup. She and I regularly wander the aisles picking out outrageous colors for our lips, eyes, and nails, to my mother's dismay. I am not allowed to wear makeup because obviously wearing makeup leads to having sex with boys and my eventual unwanted pregnancy, which then raises questions about abortion, which is absolutely forbidden because we are a good Catholic family. My mother gets all this from a $1 bottle of Wet n Wild hot-pink nail polish Grandma buys me at Woolworths. But this is how my mother's brain works—she is like a Catholic Lamborghini that goes from wearing nail polish straight to my impending abortion in six seconds flat.

Some of my favorite moments are when Grandma lets me explore the colorful riches that lay across her dresser. I try on all of her jewelry, most of which is fake but from the 1920s, so amazing. I drape myself in her necklaces and bracelets and clip-on earrings. This is perfect because I am also not allowed to have my ears pierced until I am practically in college. Occasionally she lets me spritz myself with her various perfumes, which are lined up in their pretty, colorful glass bottles next to the jewelry. My favorite is a royal blue crystal bell with a long silver handle.

I do all of this under a very particular watchful eye.

At the center of the dresser is my grandmother's prize possession: The Infant of Prague.

The Infant of Prague is Baby Jesus dressed in the enormous flowing robes of a king. On Jesus's head, he wears a tall, pointy, jeweled hat, and in his left hand he holds a globe with a cross on top. His right hand is raised in a sign of benediction. The image is beyond opulent, it's exultant and lavish and bejeweled. Given how much my grandmother loves sparkly things, it makes sense she would also love a sparkly Jesus in a fancy outfit.

Grandma's particular version of the Infant of Prague is a statue about a foot and a half tall, and Jesus's kingly robes are made of actual red velvet, the fur trim white and fuzzy like the stuffed animals on my bed. Better even than Jesus's touch-and-feel robes is the fact that Grandma's Infant of Prague sits under a giant dome of glass to protect it from the elements, a dome she regularly dusts and Windexes. Every day, my grandmother gets up, gets dressed, and puts on her jewelry, perfume, and makeup, poufing her hair while King Baby Jesus looks on.

This is the one thing in Grandma's room I am not, under any circumstances, allowed to touch. Not the glass dome and definitely not the statue sitting underneath it. But like everything else of Grandma's, I come to love and admire it. As with the "Footprints" poem that sits atop my mother's television set while I watch Tom and Jerry and the Road Runner as a child, the Infant of Prague presides over all of my time with my grandmother, whether I'm keeping her company while she irons and watches her soaps, or she is teaching me to powder my cheeks and spritz my wrist.

"You are our miracle, Donna," my mother is saying. She often tells the story of my birth, and for this telling, we're in the car on our way to school. "Your father and I had given up hope, then one day you arrived."

I'm in first grade or maybe second, and we drive together because she is a teacher and I am a student. I'm wearing my dark-blue-and-green plaid uniform skirt. It's pleated with a pinafore attached, a pale-yellow button-down shirt underneath it.

Back then, all schools were Catholic as far as I knew, and all teachers were Catholic, like my mother and her teacher friends. Growing up in the '70s and '80s, the nuns were all over the place in my life—teaching, singing, showing my peers and me how to look into microscopes, and most likely, the nuns were the principals, too.

As a child, I don't mind the nuns. I like the nuns. There are a few infamous ones, the kind out of the movies, stern and scary, prone to harsh punishments. Sister Helen is the worst, but I end up having her in second grade anyway. For the most part, though, the nuns who populate my world are full of humor, kindness, and friendship where my mother is concerned, wonderful ladies in their thick-soled practical shoes and infinitely appropriate skirt hems that reach below the knee, long habits cascading down their backs. Nuns are at our church and my school of course, but they're also at my house and downtown at the supermarket and definitely sitting on the beach as well. The whole world seems Catholic to me because my whole world is Catholic. All this plus the world is garishly and lavishly decorated with saints and statues of Mary everywhere.

My mother seems enormous next to me in the car, and she stares straight ahead through the windshield as she talks. "Your father and I wanted a house full of children after we got married, and for many years we hoped and prayed, but it was not to be. We went to the doctor to see what was wrong, and the doctors tried to help us, but nothing worked. Your father and I were devastated."

I am watching her drive as I listen, her short, frosted hair coiffed as usual, a colorful teacher sweater keeping her warm on this gray day. I know this story by heart, and I can probably tell it word for word myself, but I love hearing this story from my mother because it is about how I came to exist. What child wouldn't? Often what prompts the telling of my birth story is me asking my mother for a sister or a brother because I am an only child. At night I pray before bed, and I'm always asking God for a sibling. I ask God, I ask my parents, I even ask my grandmother, yet the answer is always, sadly, no. Today isn't any different, I've asked my mother if possibly a brother or sister is on the way right now as we drive in the car, and she is explaining why not. Again.

I want a sibling so badly that not long before this car ride, there was a show-and-tell incident at school where, when show-and-tell was about to end and the teacher was asking if anyone else had something to offer the class, I piped up, "I do!"

I'm not sure what possessed me to say what I did next, but boy, did it cause a ruckus. I got up from my mat and stood at the front of the room amid the circle of my fellow classmates, very excited to share some news. "No one else knows this," I began, heart pounding as the words fell from my mouth. "But soon I am going to have a baby brother or baby sister!"

Yes, dear reader, I announced to my whole class that my mother was pregnant, and no, dear reader, she was not. In my child's brain,

I believed if I spoke it out loud, I could somehow make it so. Perhaps if I told the world I was going to have a sibling, one would magically arrive. I could *will* my mother to be pregnant. Simply claiming a baby was on the way seemed like it could work and I was open to trying anything. Besides, my mother was constantly praying out loud for things and then telling me how her prayers were answered. This was my way of following her lead. She petitioned the saints and they responded, so I petitioned everyone who could hear me—my little classmates, the stuffed animals in the corner, and whatever saints might be around in the classroom at the moment, listening in on our show-and-tell.

I remember the look on my teacher's face after I made my grand announcement—my teacher who was also my mother's colleague and friend—how it lit up with surprise and happiness.

"What exciting news, Donna," she said. "How wonderful!"

School ended and my mother came to pick me up. By then the word had spread among the teachers that my mother was pregnant. People were congratulating her as she walked down the hallway toward the other end of the building, and she was very confused as to why. But she soon found out the reason when she arrived at my classroom.

My teacher greeted her at the door. "Donna told us your news during show-and-tell today!"

"What news?" my mother asked.

The other parents picking up their kids surrounded her, offering their congratulations and pulling her into hugs. I could feel my mother's laser eyes on me, and my stomach churned. I both knew and also wasn't sure if what I had done was wrong, and I really did have this hope that maybe my words spoken out loud to a whole bunch of people would somehow place a baby in my mother's stomach. The moment of truth had arrived.

My teacher clasped her hands in front of her chest, eyes dancing. "Donna is very excited for the arrival of a baby brother or baby sister!"

Only now as an adult do I understand the terrible position in which I put my mother, announcing to her colleagues and the world around us that she was going to have another baby—something my mother deeply longed for but was never to be. How painful it must have been for her to correct everyone on my behalf, explain that I didn't understand what I had done, that I also held my own deep longings for a sibling and could not seem to accept these longings were never to be fulfilled. My mother would not have any more children, no matter how she hoped and prayed.

On the way home that day, she was not happy with me. It was a tense evening at the dinner table as she told my father and grandmother what I had done. But of course, my mother forgave me. She understood that my intentions were good.

So on our way to school on yet another morning, my mother is explaining both how I came to exist and why I am an only child. She is talking about her marriage to my father, how many long years they were together before my arrival.

"Our ten-year anniversary passed, then our eleventh, and still we had no sign of a baby," she says. "So your father and I decided we would try to adopt. But then, just before we celebrated our twelfth anniversary, your mother found out she was pregnant."

"With me," I offer.

She smiles as she turns the wheel, getting ready to take the on-ramp to our right, the school a mile ahead. "Yes, with you. Your father and I were overjoyed. After all those years of hoping and praying, God answered our prayers, and what an answer he gave us." She is still smiling as she says this, because I am apparently an excellent answer from God. This is good news because I am a handful already. I'm glad she seems happy to keep me, despite this.

By now we are pulling into the school's entrance and my mother is beginning the long loop around the building and the fields where we play for recess, heading toward the teacher parking lot. Just in time, because the story is almost over. My mother pulls into the first space near the door because we are often the first people to arrive at school, the only other person there before us is the principal, also a nun, a really nice one and my mother's good friend.

She turns the key in the ignition and the car goes silent. She looks at me and I look at her, waiting for the story's grand finish. "Twelve years, sweetheart. Your father and I waited twelve long years for you," she says, never tiring of telling me this. "Every day I get up in the morning and thank God for you because you are our miracle, sweetheart. God sent us a miracle and it was you."

Then we get out of the car and head into school to start our day.

What's important to understand about growing up in a Catholic world like mine—with Italian Roman Catholic women like my mother and grandmother at the helm of it, and where one of those women prayed for twelve years not only to God and Jesus but every saint tangentially relevant to getting pregnant—is that displaying statues like King Baby Jesus under a dome of glass is only the beginning.

The Catholic saints are a regular part of life, be it on the mass cards lying around the kitchen and in my mother's room, or with the smaller statues of saintly men and women that my mother and grandmother venerate on a daily basis. And of course, there is the Virgin Mary, too, a particular favorite of my mother's and of so many devout Catholics.

So amid the flower beds and the pots and pans and all across the rooms where I play with Legos and read *The Mouse and the Motorcycle*, where I learn my letters and numbers and do my homework from the Catholic elementary school I attend, the saints and symbols of my family's faith are ever-present in a physical sense everywhere I look, a normal part of the décor. Maybe even more indelible are the sounds that accompany these childhood companions, the talking and praying to the saints and Mary for the things we need most or have lost or for which we are so very grateful. My mother especially holds a running conversation with St. Anthony, always talking to him out loud, in the kitchen, the car, the yard. Anthony is forever of service.

For Italian people, St. Anthony is the standout star of sainthood, kind of like the Frank Sinatra of saints, the go-to for just about anything you could need. Anthony is useful and all-encompassing, the Finder of Lost Things and, like St. Jude, one of the Patron Saints of Last Resort. You can call on Anthony for lost keys or even a lost pair of pants, as well as more serious things like a lost pet, or even the loss of a child, a parent, a husband, a wife.

One of my strongest St. Anthony memories has to do with my father's wedding ring.

Every other Saturday my dad would cut the grass. It was a big deal when my parents decided to invest in a rider mower to make cutting the lawn less cumbersome, the kind with a grass catcher. Now, instead of pushing the old, rusty mower with the manual, rotary blade, my dad would drive around the yard until the grass catcher was full, then lug it over to the vacant lot behind our house to empty it amid the tall grasses. I often helped him do this, eager to earn a dollar that I could later use to buy the books I was constantly gobbling in all my spare time.

This particular Saturday, like always, my father finished the lawn, then drove the mower back into the garage. Saturday night arrived and it grew dark. My parents were watching television in the living room after we finished dinner, and I was at the kitchen table playing cards with Grandma.

Suddenly my father was up from the couch, frantic. "My wedding ring is gone!"

He had been sitting there peacefully when his gaze traveled to his hand. The familiar gold band that represented more than two decades of marriage to my mother was absent. He knew immediately what must have happened, that it probably fell off while he was mowing the lawn, maybe as he was releasing the grass catcher from the machine or lugging it—gulp—toward the empty lot out back. He assumed this symbol of his love for my mother was gone forever.

We all did. Our hearts sank.

Except for my mother. "Everyone needs to pray to St. Anthony," she told us. Then very loudly, into the ether, she called to him. "St. Anthony, you need to help us find Ray's ring!"

Out came the flashlights, and the four of us filed into the yard through the sliding glass doors of the kitchen. We began our search in the pitch darkness, traveling up and down the grass in long, careful lines, like we were mowing the lawn all over again. We bent low, flashlights pointed toward the ground, eyes straining, hoping for a miracle. I could hear my mother praying to St. Anthony the entire time, murmuring a never-ending petition.

Even at the age of nine or ten, I was sure our effort was doomed. How were we going to find my father's wedding ring in the vastness of the yard? Or worse, in the vacant lot with all that tall grass? In the *dark*? Anything could have happened to that ring. A bunny could have ingested it and hopped off with my father's wedding band in his tummy. But we searched anyway, up and down the yard, while my father plowed his way through the mountain of grass in the vacant lot behind us. A fool's mission. The four of us were outside at least an hour when my mother began to shout.

"I found it! I've got it! Thank you, Anthony! Anthony, you came through for us again!" In my mother's hand was my father's shiny gold ring, in her eyes, plenty of tears. Maybe for the found ring, but maybe for the way Anthony had answered her call like always.

My heart pounded as I stood there in the yard.

That memory of my mother shouting so triumphantly is burned into me. I can hear her voice, even now. I can put myself back into the darkness and the chill of the evening air, hear the blades of grass sliding under my feet and the crickets singing in the quiet, see the beams of the flashlights cutting across the night as we searched, then my father rushing over to his wife as she shouted, a shadow moving, the outline of my mother, the gold ring held high. And I can remember feeling wondrous. What had happened out here, on this night? Was it sheer luck or something more powerful and divine that occurred? Had my mother—in her absolute faith—stirred St. Anthony to action, had he intervened and guided her to the exact right spot where my father's wedding ring awaited, rewarding her with the unlikeliest of successes? What would have happened if I'd petitioned Anthony instead? Would he have answered or ignored me?

I've never had the guts to ask St. Anthony for anything. Not then, not now. Not like my mother. My whole life I listened to her talk to Anthony and so many other saints, as simply and casually as if she was asking me what I'd like for breakfast or dinner. She talked to them like they were in the room, ready to sit down for pancakes with us at the kitchen table. Like she could see them as clearly as she could see me, her own daughter. Maybe for her, the saints were that present, that evident in our house, in the air and all around us. Everywhere she went, they were with her, ready and waiting to hear her call.

As I watched my mother pray out loud while she wandered the yard searching for my father's ring, or even as she was cooking pasta and meatballs for dinner, my mother was imparting another gift that would later become a source of grace to me, long after I was an adult and began to admire her faith in a way I couldn't appreciate as a child. As she spoke to Anthony and Jude and Joseph before dropping me off at a high school dance or traveling the aisles of the supermarket, she was throwing me yet another lifeline, one that would eventually help me to pick up the pieces of one lost career to trade it for another: she was teaching me to talk to the dead.

6

God is everywhere.

A t the heart of Narragansett, where I spend the entirety of my childhood, are its beaches. This is the real reason my family moves there, why my mother wants us to live in this small Rhode Island town. Tiny sailboats floating across oceans, bridges, and more bridges. Coastline everywhere. The sea like glass in the morning.

My mother loves the beach like she loves her garden, like she loves to perform her alchemy in the kitchen when she is cooking with my grandmother, like she adores the children that clamor for her hugs each day at the nursery school where she teaches. All these things—ocean, food, Catholic school and its children, its teacher-nuns—she loves them because they are her grace, her signs that God is everywhere, that she can't turn even a little without bumping into proof that God is with us in everything we do and are and everywhere we go. But especially God is in the sand and the surf.

My mother's school year ends in June, and while she loves her little students, she lives for the ocean. My childhood summers consist of getting up as early as the sun; packing a cooler full of snacks, fruit, lunches; gathering my pails and shovels; feet slipping into flip-flops. Off my mother and I go, Grandma with us. We are out of the house and on our way by 7:00 a.m., 8:00 at the latest, often the first ones on the beach. We have our pick of spots, and my mother has her favorite place to sit, right between one of the lifeguard chairs and the ocean's edge. Out go the chairs and towels and up go the umbrellas, one an orange-and-white pinwheel, the other a solid blue. First on the agenda is a walk, especially if the tide is low and it's left behind many piles of treasure. I am on the hunt for sea glass and my mother helps me search. We move toward the end of the beach where the hermit crabs scurry in the tide pools, another popular destination on our walks. But hunting for sea glass is serious business and I must cover every inch of ground, so our progress is painstakingly slow. Afterward, it's time for a swim, especially when the water is calm. Over the course of the day as the wind picks up, the waves will churn and rise and crash, but in the mornings there are often only tiny, clear ripples. My mother and I love it when we can see our toes at the bottom.

The morning wanes, other people trickle in and set up their things. Soon our spot has grown to include my mother's teacher friends and their children, who become my friends as we get older together. Our searches for clams and green crabs and the building of dribble castles will eventually give way to suntanning and boy-watching and getting up the nerve to talk to one of our crushes.

My mother's best beach-loving friend is an ex-nun with whom she went to college. My mother's life is full of both nuns and ex-nuns, not only because of the Catholic school where she works, but because she went to college at a place that trained young nuns back in the '50s and '60s, many of whom never made it to a convent because they met someone and fell in love before they could. My mother's stories of attending this "glorified nun school" involve being packed into large rooms set up with rows of cots, where she would sleep alongside all the other nuns-in-training. So occasionally nuns from her school or nuns from my mother's past will arrive to sit with us on the sand and enjoy the sun and surf.

In my imagination, I can go back and see those women on the beach, go down the line and count them out: ex-nun, nun, my mother, surrounded by the rest of us, the children.

Each day of summer, rain or shine, we go to that beach of my childhood, and each night after my father gets off work, he comes to meet us there for a few hours, until the sun goes down and the beach grows dark. He often picks up pizza on the way and we will sit and eat together with my mother's holdout friends, who haven't left the beach yet, either. Cheese oozes onto sweatshirts that ward against the chill, everyone happily munching as we stare at the ocean in the twilight. My father convinces me we should go for a swim, despite the cooler air. We are the first people there in the morning and often the last to leave at night.

My mother is as devoted to the beach as she is to God and her saints, though for her they are all intermingled. God is as close when she is walking the sand or wading into the water as God is in the church where we attend mass on Sundays and where she stops by during the week to sit in a pew and say a rosary or two. She has always believed that God resides in every living, breathing thing and in all the world's natural beauty, and freely expresses this belief each time I find an exciting new creature at the tide pools, or when we wade into the water together. She's so unconflicted about God's presence, she doesn't doubt it ever. William James would have no trouble categorizing my mother—she's as healthy-minded when it comes to faith as a person can be.

I learn to think of the ocean as its own kind of church, one that swirls around my ankles, my legs, my body as my mother and father and I tiptoe into the Atlantic, trying to master the water's chill so we can dive under. For my family this beach is equal to if not greater than the church building, with its stained glass windows and tall, wood-beamed ceilings. So it seems like destiny when, decades later, my father and I lay my mother to rest in this place where she enjoyed so many days of summer; that someone like my mother deserves to spend eternity on this one stretch of sand and in this ocean that made her so happy.

This is the rhythm of my childhood life. My whole family and I dance to the tune of faith.

Beach, beach, and more beach during summer, school, teaching, homework, cooking, and family meals in winter. Mingled into all the seasons will be Bible reading, other reading, prayer before bed, always involving one parent or the other engaging in these activities. There will be church on Sundays, sometimes Sunday school, too, then Sunday afternoon post-church lunch, which is always special, always an event, always long and delicious.

Catholicism is not just a faith tradition for my family, it is a culture. The culture is all around me, and even if I eventually don't believe its tenets or have faith in its God, I am still a part of it. I have no choice but to be a part of it. Everyone I know is Catholic, the symbols of it are everywhere, and its people are my family and my family's friends and colleagues.

My mother is the leader of its overall rhythms, but my father is the one prone to taking down the big, tall children's Bible that sits on one of the walnut bookshelves in our living room, shelves my grandpa built, next to the many volumes of our encyclopedia. The children's Bible has two big lions drawn on the cover in colorful charcoal pencil, a female and a male. Jesus stands tall above them in a persimmon-colored tunic, hands outstretched above the lions' heads, which today makes me laugh, since when did Jesus ever hang out with lions? But more than Jesus, I remember those roaring, majestic creatures because they seemed so exciting at the time, and I remember my father and I talking together about all the pictures and the stories.

"Sweetheart, come here," he says in the evening after dinner, already up off the couch and headed to the shelf where my special Bible lives, pulling it out. We sit down next to each other and open to one of the stories so we can read it out loud and talk about it.

When it is time for bed, either my mother or my father does the honors of helping me to get ready, brush my teeth and such, then sit with me at the side of my bed to pray while I get under the covers. Popular topics involve thanking God for our food, our house, and each other, special prayers for both grandmas and my grandpa, occasionally for my teachers, and a few friends.

As the seasons go round, summer to fall, fall to winter, I also pray that Santa will bring me a Barbie Dreamhouse, please. Or a Barbie car. Or something exciting from FAO Schwarz, the toy store my parents brought me to as a special treat on a visit to New York City to see the Rockettes Christmas extravaganza (Grandma's idea). I become obsessed with the place, and surely my parents regret allowing me to know it exists. After this trip, I get their catalog and read through it carefully, marking all the things I hope will suddenly arrive at the house on Santa's sleigh, writing Santa long lists that go on for pages. I take one of the yellow lined pads from my parents' big wooden desk and fill those pages with my awkward handwriting in pencil. My father tolerates my asking God for toys at the end of my prayers, but my mother is never happy about this tendency of mine.

"We do not ask God for *things*," she admonishes.

I often think, *But why? I want a Barbie Dreamhouse and God should know!*

The one hitch in the pleasant rhythm of our Catholic household, regardless of the time of year, occurs on Fridays. Fridays are when we eat fish, and not only Fridays during Lent like most Catholics in the '70s and '80s, but every Friday of the year. I learn quickly I hate fish. I may grow up by the sea and happily eat the tiny clams my mother loves to steam, or watch as my father cracks open a lobster claw so I can follow his lead, but fish is another story and it's unfortunate for me that we are Catholic. I specifically hate the fish my incredibly talented cook of a mother makes for us. Steam-baked with breadcrumbs and lemon in the oven. Flounder, always flounder. When I say always, I mean that until I am in college and study abroad in Chile, where people eat a lot of fish—lots of different kinds of fish—I literally don't know there are many types of fish. I actually think all fish is flounder and it is always cooked in the same way—in a Pyrex baking dish in a big wet pile of yuck. The first time I taste sea bass and salmon, I am stunned and I am also an adult.

So as a child, Friday always looms large and ominous because I know what awaits me at dinnertime—a battle of wills at the table with my mother, a kind of holy war in our house on a weekly basis. My mother not only teaches me that we do not pray for *things*, but she also loves to remind me that not everyone is lucky enough to have food on their table, and loves to use that royal "we," while giving me the stink eye.

"*We* do not leave food behind on our plates in this house."

There are no dogs or cats to feed under the table, since my father and I are both allergic. So I sit there in the kitchen on Friday evenings, first accompanied by Mom, Dad, and Grandma, then eventually alone, because everyone else has long since finished their dinners and moved on to their nightly reading or television-watching or puttering around playing solitaire or gin rummy. Meanwhile my horrific plate of fish has grown cold. Eventually my mother begins to bargain with me. Five bites and I can be done. Five bites more is not a lot to ask, is it?

I always try to knock it down to four bites, then three, then two.

Fish on Fridays aside, the faith that threads my family's life together is as ordinary as dressing for school each day, as riding my bike through the neighborhood or getting into the car to accompany my dad to the barbershop on a Saturday, or packing the cooler in summer to head off for an endless day by the ocean. It is everywhere I look and in everything we do as a family. Faith and me and us are seamless. The stuff of life. It is always there.

I know why I begin this story here—in the house where I grew up and on the beaches of Narragansett, where I will one day marry my first husband and a decade later mourn the loss of our marriage. This is the setting where I lost my faith, so if I am a good enough conjurer, maybe I can see where it got to, empty just the right pocket and watch as it falls to the floor, amid the tiny, sparkling grains of sand from the shells I've collected on a walk. Maybe it's still waiting for me to see it there, and possess it again for myself. Or it's hidden within one of the many blankets my grandmother crocheted for me, my faith a missed stitch amid the rest of it. I only have to go back to the source of the error and pick up the thread again, redo the tapestry but this time, replete with belief.

As I call up these memories of my mother and grandmother, their voices talking to the saints, so many petitions and prayers and nuns and so much talk of God, I can't help but see what's there. Faith was all around me all of the time, my mother an endlessly willing conversation partner at my side, unfazed by my anxieties, questions, my doubts about God, Jesus, how this whole faith thing works. But it was also always sliding off me, unwilling to stick, to sink in, my skin rejecting it rather than absorbing it. I don't know why. But I want to.

7

Oh, how I love Jesus.

The church where we go to mass is a ten-minute drive down the road that snakes along the water in Narragansett. The building is small and old, but serviceable, at least before it's renovated to be shiny and modern many years later when I'm an adult and planning my mother's funeral. It's called St. Thomas More, a typical name for a typical Catholic parish. I'm always trying to get out of attending mass, and I am always failing at getting out of attending. My mother cannot be bought, not by any of my efforts.

I am bored by the long, unending service, listening to fellow parishioners drone on as they read word for word from the mass books in the pews, prayers repeated week after week that I learn by heart because it's impossible not to. Worse still, my mother likes us to sit in the front row if it's open, right under the noses of the priest and deacons and altar boys. Sometimes the priest glares at me during his sermon because I am always restless. One of the lowest points of my childhood mass attendance involves the priest stopping his homily to tell me to sit still in front of the entire congregation. I will never forget the moment when Father Hogan does this to me. But mostly I sit safely off to the side of my family and out of the sight line of the priest so I can stare at Jesus. He lives in an alcove at the front of our church and I am fascinated by him.

Jesus is gigantic, bloody, and hanging on the cross. His expression is one of agony, the crown of thorns piercing his forehead and skin, graphically so. I take in his every detail. The spikes through Jesus's hands and feet, the height of the cross on which he hangs. The wound at his chest, the blood dripping down from the seam of it. It's hard to look away so I don't. I find his body, his situation, grotesque and riveting. I ponder him week after week, year after year as I get older, trying to understand why this bloody, dying man serves as the heart of my family's faith tradition. Why would someone do this to a person? Why do we celebrate that such things were done? What in the world is this religion about? I am most perplexed by Easter, and I ask my mother over and over why Good Friday is good if it's also the day they did this to Jesus. No matter how she explains or tries to make me understand, none of it makes sense.

"Good Friday is good because Jesus must die on the cross in order to rise from the dead," she'll say to me in one way or the other, over the course of many Easters—until I am old enough to stop asking such questions, and I've washed my hands of my family's faith tradition altogether.

But as a child, I try hard to grasp concepts that elude me even now. I shake my head at her as I think of the gigantic, bloodied Jesus at the front of our church, the expression of defeat and agony on his face. It doesn't add up.

"Couldn't this have happened another way?" I'll ask my mother next, and she will try to explain it to me yet again.

Now I am stomping around the house, singing, "Ohhh, how I love Jesus! Ohhh, how I love Jee-eee-zaahh-aahhs!" I have a terrible voice, but I love belting out my love for Jesus, specifically that second line, where your voice is meant to go really high and you're supposed to draw out Jesus's name into way more syllables than it actually has. Four-syllable Jesus.

I am cruising around through the living room, the family room, onward around the kitchen island, airplaning my arms as I repeat these lines over and over, shouting them from my loud child's mouth, while Grandma and Mom are at the stove, cooking. One of the many songs I know from church, Sunday school, from my mother, who taught me to sing it.

My mother is often in the kitchen, teaching me how to make a sauce, meatballs, homemade pasta, while chatting with me about what I'm reading, my favorite classes, what makes me stuck on my homework. Soon we will all be singing—she, Grandma, and I together. *Michael, row the boat ashore, halleluuuyahhh!* Eventually we might come back to the recipes, how to know when a dish is just right or needs another herb, a pinch of this, onward again to discussing school. The typical soundtrack of a weekday afternoon.

I sing my way to the mailbox on behalf of my mother's request to go and check it. Probably to get me out of the house for five minutes and experience a bit of peace and quiet. After I retrieve the mail, I zoom back into the house, still yelling, my mother laughing at my zest. She is stirring a big pot of sauce during this memory. I put the mail on the counter, after which my grandma slips me raw cloves of garlic to eat, because she does that a lot. To ward off evil spirits and also because Grandma believes garlic can cure anything. She is always clipping articles about the miracle of garlic from her favorite papers, the *National Enquirer* and the *Star*, and leaving them on the table or the kitchen island so we can read them.

But I sing of my love for Jesus because my mother lets me sing this as loud as I want, a special perk. She's happy to hear me say I love Jesus over and over, because this is what she feels for Jesus and she wants it for me, too. I feel like I am getting away with something because if the subject was any different, say, if I was singing *Billie Jean is not my lover*, she would tell me to lower my voice, ask me to stop stomping my feet so hard on the floor, to not run and zoom and airplane my arms, to not be such a hyper child. So singing about loving Jesus liberates me to be me, to let my voice shake my body and reverberate through my rib cage, to let me take flight and somehow, at the very same time, make my mother laugh and laugh.

As a child, I am afraid of the dark. As an adult, I still am.

To ward off the fear, I have a night-light. It is a bunch of balloons, big and plastic and hollow, red and orange and yellow and pink and blue, maybe two feet tall. At the center is a lightbulb. Each night it gets turned on and I stare at the shadows it creates on the wall.

My parents always tuck me in. I remember my father by my side, night after night, talking until I fall asleep. My fear is gaping, endless, and it makes my parents worry deeply.

I remember entire years of childhood when my father stayed with me until I slept, or wouldn't sleep. My parents tried all kinds of things to calm me about the dark, moved my bed around, rearranged the furniture, the shelves. Nothing worked. I remember piling every stuffed animal in my room onto my bed, surrounding myself with every bunny and walrus and Raggedy Ann, lining them up under the covers with me in the middle.

If my father leaves before I am truly asleep, I open my eyes after he's gone and stare through the gap in the curtains at the stars. The enormity of the sky, its accompanying beauty, frightens me. Its vastness makes me feel like a speck and I wonder what might come for me. If it isn't the sky, I position myself so I can see down the hallway leading up to my room. Another night-light is plugged in by the bathroom, casting a glow over the floorboards and creating shadows. I wait for someone to turn the corner, someone bad. If it isn't this, I stare at the flowers on my wallpaper, woozy with the petals that seem to expand and contract as I watch them.

I remember feeling so out of control in the quiet of the night, brain churning, unwilling to give me any peace. I never know how to make my mind stop. My parents watch, helpless, as my eyes widen full of fear, and my hand shoots out, reaching for them when they get up to tiptoe out of my room.

"Don't go," I plead. "Not yet."

I am so lonely inside, even then.

In kindergarten, my faith is tested again. Nearly all of my earliest memories have to do with church, belief, God, how and why things work the way they do, why we are made the way we are. But this time, the subject is my love for Jesus.

"Do *you* love Jesus?"

I am sitting at the table during snack with the rest of my tiny classmates, and a boy there with us, a known troublemaker, has just asked me this question. I look at him, I blink, but I don't answer—not yet.

The kindergarten is called Lily Pads, and like everything else in my life, it's Catholic, so Jesus, God, all the kid-oriented stories from the Bible like Jonah being swallowed by the whale are popular fare. We talk and sing about Jesus, just like at home. But when this boy asks about my love for Jesus while munching his graham crackers, mouth wide open revealing the grossness inside it, I hesitate. Not because I don't know what to say—the response, at the time, is easy and it's a yes. But even at my tender age I can sense that his question is a trick. He is setting me up somehow. But for what, I don't know; I can't figure it out.

Other people at the snack table are also waiting for my answer. My hesitation only makes things worse.

I've been having a good day thus far. One of my favorite things about Lily Pads is the aluminum-foil-covered mock-up of the space shuttle in the corner of the room, with its knobs and dials and buttons pasted onto it. We line up to play in it, vie for turns at the shiny thing to pretend we are astronauts going to the moon. I've just had my time in it and I'm still glowing with the privilege. Maybe this boy is mad since he's always losing his turn because of his antics, and he's punishing me for being the kind of good kid allowed to play in the mock space shuttle. Whatever his reason, something is coming and I know it isn't good.

As I watch this boy munch his graham crackers, I become slightly panicked about telling him that yes, I do love Jesus. But what else can I possibly say? What else can anyone possibly say? Don't we all love Jesus? Doesn't everyone in the world love Jesus?

"Of course I love Jesus," I finally tell the boy.

His sneer is immediate. Uh-oh.

"So are you going to marry him then?"

A bunch of other kids at the table snicker and laugh.

My shame is instant, it burns my little cheeks. My whole face, my whole body is on fire. The intensity of the shame is why I remember this moment so vividly—enough that I can see the blue Formica top of the table, the faces of the other kids watching me, the teacher's desk in the periphery of my vision. At the time, I'm not sure why I am so unnerved and embarrassed, all I know is I am supposed to love Jesus, but I am not supposed to marry him. I've intuited there is something different about the love we are meant to have for Jesus, and the love, say, between my parents. I don't yet know what the difference entails, but I feel it in my gut. I also know the insinuation this boy makes about me marrying Jesus is somehow wrong, though I don't know why or how yet, either.

So I have no idea how to answer this boy's latest question. People who love each other get married, like my parents and friends' parents. So what is the answer? What if I say no, I don't want to marry Jesus, and it's wrong? Or what if I say no and it makes people question my love for Jesus? I've been raised to love Jesus, so why shouldn't I marry him? Like everything else in my young life, I can't let anything be simple.

My classmates are still waiting for my answer, too.

"No, I'm not going to marry Jesus!" I finally snap.

But inside I'm uncertain and filled with dread.

"Why not?" the boy sneers again. "You said you loved him!"

"I do love him," I confirm.

"So then why don't you want to marry him?"

I don't know, I don't know. It's a trap, this boy has set a trap and my short legs are caught in its sharp jaws. I don't say anything now because I have no idea how to get out of this situation. The kids around me are laughing and my body is burning and Miss Pat (yes, that is her name, I know it sounds like a joke, but my teacher is actually named Miss Pat) is hurrying over to find out about the ruckus. She already knows who's behind it because he's behind every issue in our classroom. Mercifully, Miss Pat doesn't push too hard to find out why the kids are laughing at me, so I escape further humiliation. But his stupid question lingers in me long afterward.

When I get home from school, I am still unnerved. I am racked with guilt, confusion, shame. My mother can tell. She presses me about what's the matter.

"If I love Jesus, am I supposed to want to marry him?" I ask her.

My mother bursts into laughter. "No, sweetheart."

"But *why*?"

"Because the love between married people is different," she tells me.

Okay. Because I've already sensed this is the case, I am calmed by her confirmation that my answer at the snack table was correct, but she doesn't explain *how* this love is different. I don't ask her to expand, either, even though I still want to understand how everything works, how we distinguish one kind of love from another; to understand the role of this Jesus person so present in our lives, whose pictures are everywhere I look at home, in framed portraits and on the cover of books, whose name is always falling from the lips of my family, yet who never comes over for dinner and whom I've never met in person. Like all the cooking and singing that goes on in my house, the talk of saints and God, Jesus is pumped through the breath in my lungs and sung through the cavern of my mouth, and he is always on the tip of my tongue. So early on in my life, Jesus is in my heart completely and totally and all of the time. Until one day, not too long from now, he will begin his departure.

8

Boys in the pews, holes in my shoes.

I am in love. His name is Davey. He has brown floppy hair, big brown eyes. The most beautiful face I've ever seen. He is older than me, which means he's tall and totally swoonworthy. He is also my mother's Sunday school helper. This is obviously a match made in heaven.

At the time, I am probably eight or nine, and maybe Davey is twelve? I'm only masquerading as a believer at this point, living a lie in my own home, because my young heart is plagued with doubt and disbelief after my discovery a few years before that there are many gods. Yet I am living among devout Catholics, whose lives revolve around church in every way, so I go along with everything they do. Also, my mother gives me no choice.

When I resist anything to do with mass or prayer, my mother shakes her head. "When you go through the sacrament of Confirmation, your faith will be yours and you can determine whether to go to church," she says. "But you are not Confirmed yet, Donna Marie Angelina, so you are coming with us to mass." End of story.

Lucky for me, Sunday school is infinitely more appealing now that my mother has hired Davey as her assistant. Hired might be a strong term for the situation, though. I don't think Davey is getting paid, and my mother probably just plucked him from the pews one day because of his amazingly strong arms, and she needed someone to carry a stack of hymnals to the Sunday school room. Either way, suddenly Davey is on my mother's weekly agenda, and suddenly I am game for all things church.

My mother is suspicious of this turn of events, especially when she finds me dressed, ready, and eager on a Sunday morning, waiting for her in the kitchen.

"Can I go to Sunday school with you this week?" I ask. "Instead of mass?"

She returns my question with this stare she has, eyes narrowed, lips pursed. There is a pregnant pause. She is already wondering about my motives. Church and Jesus are the way to my mother's heart, and I am doing my best to use this to my advantage—my romantic advantage. One way or another on Sundays, our family piles into my father's car and heads down to St. Thomas More. It's not like I can stay home alone. I'm still too young and my mother wouldn't let me anyway.

"Maybe I'll like Sunday school better than mass?" I try.

She keeps staring at me, silent.

My heart is pounding in anticipation. *Davey, Davey, Davey*, my heart says as we stand there in this face-off. My romance with Davey is on the line and I know this.

But my mother can see a scam from a mile away. Prior to this Sunday, my mother has already tried—and failed—to convince me to go to Sunday school with her. She'll try anything to get me interested in our faith, especially now that it's clear I am falling away.

But stupid me, I've vigorously declined her overtures. No wonder she's suspicious about why I've suddenly changed my mind. I can practically see the ticker tape in her brain scrolling across her forehead, as we engage in this kitchen battle of wills. *What happened between last week and this week to spark this change of heart, Donna Marie Angelina Freitas?*

But I do not offer her a reason. No way. Davey is what happened, and I will never admit this out loud. The first time I saw him was only the week before. Mass had ended and my dad and I went to help my mother pack up after Sunday school, while Grandma was off to the parking lot to socialize. When we arrived, my mother was stacking tiny carpets, tidying up the room. She was not alone. A skinny boy was helping her.

He turned.

Our eyes met.

It was love at first sight, for me, at least.

Davey was my first crush. Or I should clarify: my first real-life crush. He had some celebrity competition: Kirk Cameron and Ralph Macchio. I had it bad for Kirk and Ralph for a number of years. But soon it became Kirk, Ralph, and Davey who cycled through the revolving romantic door of my heart. That prior Sunday as my father and I stood in the doorway and my mother and her Sunday school helper finished packing up, I thought: *This is the most beautiful boy I've ever seen.* Then, I realized: *The most beautiful boy I've ever seen knows my mother.*

This was both excellent and horrible. It wasn't like I wanted to go after a boy in front of my mother. Plus, how does one go after a boy in real life? I certainly had no idea. It was one thing to long for the boys I saw on television, totally unattainable, two-dimensional figures on a screen in my living room. But Davey lived in my town, Davey went to my church! Davey and I could be in the same room together. All I knew was that I wanted to see him again, and again, and I had the perfect in to fulfill my childhood romantic longing: my mother and her Sunday school class.

"You've never been interested in Sunday school," my mother says, crossing her arms.

"Mom, please? I think I should at least try. I can help you, too." I am so sneaky with my reasoning: Davey's a helper, so I'll propose to also become my mother's helper. Then we'll get married and live happily every after!

"Fine, you can come," my mother finally agrees.

Then she turns and disappears through the door that leads to the garage.

Alas, Davey and I never end up dating. But I do discover something important about church on Sundays because of him, which helps to mitigate my resistance to going.

Boys. There are boys there. So many boys.

Boys in the pews, boys in Sunday school, boys in the communion line, boys everywhere I turn once I begin to look for them. And I do look for them, to the point that I start to view Sundays as an opportunity to feast my eyes. There are boys I know from school, boys I've never met but who apparently live nearby, who maybe attend the public school in town, or who commute to one of the private Catholic boys' schools dotting Rhode Island. I soon discover the best times for mass attendance are during summer, because then I get to see the boys from the beach up close and out of the glare of the burning sun. I become so eager to peruse the catalog of boys who show up at services that I switch the place I sit in the pew—suddenly, I am eager for an aisle seat, so when everyone gets up for communion I can see the boys who parade up the aisles with their parents. I hang over the armrest like a floppy puppy, studying everyone, thinking I am being subtle.

My grandmother cracks up at this. "What are you doing, Donna?" she asks all the time.

I return her laughing question with a horrified shake of my head, feeling caught. I've convinced myself no one in my family knows what I'm doing as I study the churchgoers, that to outside eyes it's only out of boredom that I peruse each and every person who wanders by on their way to get communion; that when I try to convince my parents to choose a new spot in the pews, they're unaware that this is because I want to be closer to my latest crush, for better viewing.

Over the years, my interest in Davey gives way to a boy named Steven, and eventually there are Andy, and Johnnie, who I know from the beach. We never acknowledge one another because none of us have ever really talked, or actually met; I just stare and stare and daydream about one of them discovering he has a crush on me, too. So while the priest drones on through the mass, my fantasies are about one of these boys realizing he is in love with me, asking me out, and one day holding my hand. Now in addition to the doubt and disbelief about God that has hatched and grown wings in my heart, suddenly the boys I see everywhere are pulling on my attention and pulling hard.

This does not go unnoticed.

Many years later I am getting ready for work. I am fifteen. It's winter and my shift begins early.

My mother is yelling through the house. "I can't believe you! I can't believe you! Donna Marie Angelina, get out here right now!"

What in the world have I done?

From the time I am old enough to get a job, when I am not at school, I'm busing tables at a restaurant my father frequents to have lunch and to watch his games. He goes there so often that the owner is willing to hire me even though I have no prior experience. On weekends, my shifts extend from early morning until late at night.

My parents want me to understand the value of work, that money is hard to make. They want me to *feel* this, on my feet, in the ache of my arms and legs and back, and I do—from ferrying trays full of steaming plates to diners and dirty dishes back into the kitchen, trays so heavy that today it seems impossible I hefted them onto my shoulders and moved them at all.

"Donna Marie Angelina!" my mother yells again.

The tone of my mother's voice makes me want to hide in the bathroom all day. The mirror is fogged and I wipe a hand across it, hurrying to brush my still-wet hair and pulling on my post-shower T-shirt and sweatpants. If I don't get a move-on, I'll be late and the head waiter is not an understanding man. Tall, like a reed, with a deep voice and short gray hair, he is always unsmiling.

I crack open the bathroom door, step outside, barefoot but dressed. "Mom?"

Her footsteps thunder in my direction. She appears in the hallway, seething, still in her nightgown and robe. In her hands she is holding something.

The penny loafers I wear to work.

My high school uniform requires certain shoes, and most of my friends and I go the penny loafer route. We'll sit on top of the heating vents in the cafeteria, trying to keep warm while we work shiny pennies into the tight leather slots, intent on going all the way with our retro footwear. Leather, flat, wine-colored, the loafers take ages to break in but then they are comfortable and I grow to love them. In truth, I grow to love my entire Catholic high school uniform, with its traditional maroon-and-white plaid skirt, white oxfords, and ugly maroon cardigan sweaters. It's a relief having my daily wardrobe chosen for me, there's a playfulness in the way my friends and I both comply with the uniform requirements and also defy them. We roll up our skirts to reveal boxer shorts underneath, wear forbidden tank tops below our oxfords to unbutton more buttons than we're allowed, head off in the morning in our thick gray tights only to take them off, bunch them up, and stuff them into our school bags to see how long we make it bare legged before a teacher threatens detention. We relish the daily battle with the hall monitors, who are sticklers for the tiniest details—the state of our socks, the length of our skirts, whether our shirts are tucked in or the tails are sticking out, if our skirts are neatly pleated or rumpled and in need of a proper ironing.

My mother thrusts the shoes in her hands toward me, breathing fire. "Explain this!"

These loafers are my castoffs, so worn out they're no longer appropriate for school, which is why I wear them for the dirty work of busing tables. The coins wedged into their fronts are dull, the leather wrinkled and sticky from the goo of hustling in a restaurant kitchen. I stare at the familiar shoes, trying to figure out what about them could make my mother so incensed. "I don't know—"

"Donna Marie Angelina, how could you?" my mother shouts.

I am shaking my head. What?

My mother flips over the offending penny loafers.

On the bottom of each one, in the center where the balls of my feet press into the soles as I walk or run or scurry, are two round matching holes, fraying at the edges. One for the left loafer, another for the right. I study these holes. But I am still confused about what, exactly, I have done. What do these holes inform my mother about me that would make her this angry? When I entered the bathroom to shower and get ready for work, my mother was fine. My work clothes were laid out on my bed—black pants, a white oxford, again a castoff from my school uniform, work loafers set on the floor nearby. For some reason, my mother found cause to give them a closer inspection.

I look up from the shoes at my mother. "What's the problem, Mom?"

She jerks them. "How can you be so careless! We do not wear shoes with holes! What will people think?"

"But, Mom, they're just for work—"

"I cannot believe that *my daughter* would leave the house like this! Have I not taught you anything? Next thing I know, you'll be pregnant and asking me to get you an abortion!"

I stare at my mother, at the red in her cheeks, the anger in her eyes. My brain is frantically parsing what has caused her to go from holes in the bottoms of my loafers to my impending pregnancy and abortion. I can also tell she's serious about every word she's said.

This is what I come up with, given what I know of my mother:

It is improper to wear shoes with holes in them. Period. More than an embarrassing sign of neglect or even poverty, it is a sign of carelessness. It communicates something about who a person is, to the world around her. A shrug—about propriety, decorum. A sign of moral laziness. Even moral defiance. My mother's upset reminds me of her other maxims in life, of the things *we do not do*, especially related to church. Among them are: we do not wear flip-flops, bathing suits under our clothing, shorts, sleeveless tops, or sleeveless dresses. I could go on.

My mother must have decided the holes in my penny loafers point toward other signs of carelessness and moral laxity on my part. She has jumped to the biggest sign of moral laxity, the worst transgression she can imagine me committing: getting pregnant as an unmarried teenager. At the time, I am still a year and a half away from my first kiss, so if a pregnancy is to occur, it will have to be immaculate, like with the Virgin Mary. I'm also on track to graduate as valedictorian of my Catholic high school. So it's my turn to grow angry now.

I snatch the shoes back from my mother, drop them to the floor in a clatter. "You don't know anything about me." I shove my feet into them, smashing the backs with my heels. "I can't believe you!" I run off to my room to put on my work outfit, my mother following after me. "You can't even see the daughter right in front of your face!" I shout.

My mother is not deterred. "All I know is that this kind of carelessness leads to other kinds of carelessness!"

An icy cold rushes through me. I have so much faith in her and yet she can't say the same for herself with me. I know just how to punish her, so I do. "I hate you and your stupid God and your stupid Church and its rules!"

Our battle has only just begun.

The clashes that occur in my house over what I want to do versus what my mother thinks is appropriate for me to do as a newly minted teenager become daily battles. She wonders where the child I was has gone. I try to tell her I'm the same person, that if she could only stop being so afraid for me, coming up with new rules to fence me in, then maybe she'd realize I've been right here all along, waiting for her to see the young woman I'm becoming, good at heart, responsible, ethical, caring.

But my mother lets her fear of my interest in boys blind her, her dismay at my choice of skirts and tops and how I want to spend my time as a young adult blind her even more—going to dances, out with friends, to the beach at night to spend time in the dunes. So I rebel. The more she tries to tighten her grip, the more I defy her rules. When she lowers my curfew, I climb out the window. When she tells me I can't hang out with someone, I lie and do it anyway.

The Catholic faith of my mother is both a thing of beauty and it's also a wedge—one that shoves us further apart when I begin to have a social life that is no longer hers to control. While as I child, my mother was happy to entertain my wonderings, as I get older, she is fearful about everything I do, who I am, how I behave. Catholicism becomes a tradition of following rules, of obedience, of being forbidden to do all kinds of things, of refraining from being curious because curiosity is dangerous. I feel its walls closing in so I scale those walls and climb right over them, I walk away and refuse to look back. My mother sees the road I'm on as full of potholes, each one full of sin, and me always on the verge of stepping into one of them, tripping and falling in a way that might break something about me that is irreparable and unredeemable.

In the future, when I get a PhD in Religion and Gender Studies, I do research about faith and young adults and see how teenagers and college students leave their traditions in droves at the same age as me, a mass exodus of Catholic youth, making my own just as predictable. But what stands out to me now is how, as a young child, the ways I pushed and tested all things Church, God, and Jesus was welcomed, but as I got older, something shifted—my doubts were no longer appreciated in the context of my faith. The resulting message seemed clear: stay Catholic and suffocate, or get out and live. I remember, too, how as a young adult, this tradition eventually stopped making me angry and resentful and instead made me feel dead. There was no room for me to breathe within it, for me to be myself, so I abandoned it like it meant nothing. Or maybe it's truer to say that it abandoned me. Either way, I felt nothing for it anymore, and wouldn't again for a very long while.

A decade later, my mother and I will talk about this time in our lives and laugh about it together; we'll come clean and I'll admit what I did and how I lied and she'll confess what she knew and we'll agree how awful it all was. We'll hug and forgive and chalk it up to me being a teenager and to her being an overly worried mother. But the damage was done all the same, and I learned to see this caution and denial of hers as rooted in the religion in which I was raised, because it is. And she would never stop worrying about it all, trying to prevent me from falling even further from the person she was trying to raise me to be. A good Catholic girl.

Not long after the fight over the penny loafers, I am Confirmed in the Catholic Church. This is a sacrament I've been waiting for, the one that will officially release me from these weekly rituals I have grown to hate, and that will bestow upon me the responsibility to be the guide of my own faith life. I am ready for it, but not in the way that my parents, my Confirmation teacher, and the priests and nuns who've populated my life are hoping. My aunt is my sponsor, I go to the Confirmation classes like I'm supposed to, but I loathe them. By now, the faltering faith of my childhood has turned to dust. I have no interest in God, Jesus, or the beliefs my mother tried so hard to instill, beliefs I no longer even attempt to understand. I do not care about any of it. Yet I go through the motions of this sacrament because I have to according to my parents, and I know my mother is holding her breath.

What will happen from here on out with my faith?

For years, my mother's been dangling Confirmation as this turning point when, afterward, I can finally decline participation in my family's regular mass attendance. So I do the thing: I get Confirmed. The one perk is I get to buy a dress I really like and will wear for years into my future—it's black, covered in tiny pink flowers, with long fitted sleeves, and a hem to the knee. For once, my mother and I manage to agree on my outfit. For Confirmation, I wear it with thick tights and ugly flats, but in the future I'll wear it with black stockings and high-heeled boots and I will feel modest yet sexy.

The first Sunday after I am Confirmed arrives. I am in my bedroom, making a point not to get dressed, remaining determinedly in my pajamas while my mother, grandma, and dad are eating breakfast and getting ready for church.

My mother keeps shuffling around outside my door, listening to see if I'm in the process of putting on my Sunday best. Instead, I am playing with my boom box, blank cassette at the ready, trying to hit *record* when one of my favorite songs comes on the radio. I spend a lot of my teenage years with my pointer finger poised over that *record* button on my yellow Sony sports cassette player, heart full of hope the next song will be the one to inspire romantic movie montages in my brain about whatever boy I am crushing on at the moment.

My mother is standing outside my room now, I can hear her breaths, her hesitation.

Then, "Sweetheart?"

"Yeah, Mom?"

"We're going to church."

"Okay!"

Pause. "Are you coming?"

Here comes the test, the moment of truth. All these years my mother has promised that post-Confirmation, the choice to go to church would be mine to make. Did she mean it?

"No, Mom," I tell her. "You guys go. I'm going to stay home."

Long pause. Then, "Okay, sweetheart. We'll see you when we get back."

I nearly stop breathing.

Can this really be?

I hear her footsteps receding down the hall, turning the corner, and moving through the living room, followed by muffled talk with my father, then everyone gathering in the kitchen and heading out. The faint sounds of the garage door opening and closing, and finally, silence.

I am alone. I have successfully avoided mass for the first time in my life.

My mother kept her word. She kept her word!

This becomes our new Sunday ritual. Me remaining in my pajamas, noodling around doing stupid things in my room, listening to American Top 40 hoping to hear my favorite songs, or watching TV, or reading the latest Sweet Valley High on the couch, to see what those teenage twins, Jessica and Elizabeth, are up to now. My family going through the motions of getting ready for mass. Eventually, my mother approaches, always hesitantly, to ask if I am coming with them to church. I always respond with the same answer: no. Week after week, she tries and I decline her invitation. To my mother's credit, she never drags me to church again. Not once. But she asks, always, throughout the rest of high school and when I return for vacations during college, and eventually when I am in my twenties and visiting for the weekend. Like before, I always give my mother the same answer: no. You go, I'll stay here. I know it hurts her deeply. I do it anyway. At the time I do not care. It turns out, my Confirmation day is the last time I will go to the church of my childhood with my family. I literally never attend mass with them again. Not until my mother's funeral.

9

And yet.

When my mother is dying of cancer during my twenties, the neighborhood carolers come by our house to sing twice on Christmas Eve—once at the start of the evening, another at the end of it. This is because my mother was their original ringleader, for years the person who organized the event—the route they took, the songs for their repertoire. Then they'd merrily go from one door to the next, singing badly but joyfully and oh so loudly while holding a bunch of printouts my mother copied with the lyrics to various Christmas favorites, from "Silent Night" and "Joy to the World" to "White Christmas" and "Here Comes Santa Claus."

But on this night, my mother is too sick to go with everyone—she can barely move across the house without help. I remember the warm Christmas lights on the tree and out in front of the house, strung across the bushes and the awning of the porch. How my father and I painstakingly try to make this Christmas seem normal, full of the usual food, the baking, the tree heavy with the ornaments collected over the years, so many of them gifts from my mother's students and their grateful parents. We put up the mistletoe in the archways and the wreath on the front door and the manger with its dozens of angels fanning out on the table. The only difference this season is my mother's energy, the way she'll put a smile on her face but you can see the exhaustion in her eyes.

Christmas was my mother's favorite time of year. For her, it was about community and sharing what we had with those around us in celebration of Jesus's birth. She would bake for weeks to make Italian cookies for the neighbors, my teachers, her colleagues, the priests at our parish. From December first onward, she would be singing one Christmas song or another as she moved across the house, as she worked in the kitchen, rolling out dough, flour everywhere. She loved Frankie Valli's renditions of all her Christmas favorites, Frank Sinatra's, too, and she tolerated my love for the Muppets Christmas record with John Denver. We'd sing the whole thing through together.

We always had an Advent calendar, sometimes big and sparkling with glitter. My mother and I would open each little cardboard door to see what lay behind it as we counted down the days until the twenty-fifth. I especially remember the years when those calendars involved candy canes or chocolates. But my mother did her best to instill in me that these prizes were beside the point, that the true spirit of Christmas was to be found in the candles lit, one by one, on the wreath above the altar at our church, to mark the weeks as we got closer to Jesus's birth; that it was for spending time with loved ones, eating together, making things with one's own hands to show the people around us we cared. Caroling with one's neighbors was also among the things that mattered most.

On this very difficult Christmas for our family, the first time the carolers knock, we are expecting them. The front yard is buried in snow and they bunch close to the house, because they know my mother can't make it far. One of her dear friends holds my mother up as she joins them to sing. But the second time we hear them knock and start to sing outside, we are surprised.

I remember one of the carolers yelling out cheerfully after my father opened the door. "We're back and we've weeded out the nonsingers!" How everyone roared with laughter, as though this was an obvious explanation for round two of songs at our house.

But we all know why they've really come back, even if no one says it out loud. They've missed my mother, her boundless energy and enthusiasm, her loud singing. Most of all, they are aware that this Christmas might be her last.

This time my father stands with my mother on the porch, wrapping her into a shawl as the carolers come closer, my mother leaning against him, too tired to go the few steps between the front door and the yard to stand among her friends and neighbors. I remember my mother raising up her voice and singing "Joy to the World," her favorite. I remember how the neighbor-carolers stayed for two more songs, until my mother could barely stand, tears rolling down the cheeks of the neighbors even as they smiled and sang with her in the cold.

My mother is the most important religious figure in my life. She was during childhood and she is still, long after her death. Throughout the twenty-nine years I was lucky enough to enjoy her energy, her hope, her zest for all things and people, especially children, she kept offering me the tools as dear to her as her trowel, her gardening gloves, that rug for her knees, her beach umbrellas and chairs and towels for lying out in the sun. Love of God, of Jesus, a belief in the power of prayer, in this notion that the communion of saints is everywhere, ready to listen and reach back if we call for help. That there are angels in heaven looking down upon us, that if we turn toward God when we are lost in the dark, God will respond with a spark of light to guide us out of the black.

I never bothered to pack those tools to take with me when I was old enough to leave the house and begin my life at college. I left them behind on purpose. To make a point to my mother that I didn't need them, didn't want them, either. I felt so righteous. The anger and disdain I held for religion, my sense of abandonment by God and all things church as a teenager was so intense, it blinded me to my mother and all that grace she held out to me in her hands.

A long time passes before I turn back to those tools once again, before I see them for the gifts they truly are. Precious, rare, special, essential. I am filled with regret that I discover their worth only after my mother's death. That it takes me decades to value the survival kit she was packing so carefully for her daughter, that has been with me all along. That by the time I realize the significance of what she offered me in life, she is no longer around to answer my questions about how all these tools work, how I might still use them, what exactly they are for and not. How they might lead me along on this rugged journey toward faith, help me claw my way out of so much darkness. I wish for her guidance, yet while she was alive, I squandered it. She was right there, but like a petulant child, I walked away without a backward glance.

Part III
The Dark Ages

10

The abyss comes for me.

I am seventeen. A freshman in college at Georgetown, the university of my dreams.

When I get my acceptance letter, I cannot believe it. When I arrive on campus, I cannot believe it. For years, I have been obsessed with Georgetown's basketball team, and my father and I would watch them during the NCAAs on the television in our living room. This is the era when Georgetown dominates college basketball, during the time of Patrick Ewing, Michael Jackson, and Jaren Jackson, when Coach John Thompson is in his prime. During my first-year move-in, I run into Patrick Ewing in the gymnasium. He is there to work with the basketball team and I can't believe what I am seeing, my hero in the flesh, a wall of a man, a giant who smiles as he heads through the lobby. I think to myself, *This is a good sign for what's to come.*

"Dad, I just saw Patrick Ewing," I tell my father, after hurrying to meet my parents to get lunch at The Tombs, the classic Georgetown bar and restaurant a block from campus.

My father beams. I have arrived in the land of basketball heaven, and we're both very happy here. Meanwhile, my mother is worried whether I will make my bed, if I'll get a good night's sleep, if I'll go out alone at night in the city. She keeps going over a list of things she believes will preserve my health and well-being during the two days they're in town to help me get settled.

Georgetown is a Catholic school, Jesuit, devoted to a liberal arts education. They require all students to study theology their first and second years of college, but this is not why I've come. I barely thought about the Catholic affiliation when I applied. My criteria for university applications included good academics, an urban location, and great basketball. My mother tried to turn me into a person of faith, but my father raised me to worship at the altar of the NCAAs, and he saw more success with his efforts. Still, my mother is thrilled to see the Jesuits in their priestly collars wandering the campus, greeting new students and their families, and she is hoping maybe Georgetown will work some magic on my faith life while I'm a student here.

My parents come to my dorm room to say good-bye before they make the long drive back to Rhode Island when their time on campus is up. My mother's face is tearstained when I open the door and see them there.

"Yup, bye!" I say, giving them quick hugs, then shooing them on their way.

I am so ready to be on my own, to not have a curfew, to not have my mother hovering over me and worrying each time I leave the house that I might return pregnant. I arrive at college having done little more than kiss a few boys from the beach in summer, and maybe a few hockey players, too. And, well, some soccer players. And maybe a baseball pitcher. But I've always been good at halting things from going too far. I enjoy making out and that is enough fun for me.

I have a good first week on campus, a good second one. Within days I have a boyfriend, the person who'll become my first love, someone I'll be with off and on until I'm a junior, someone that soon I'll think I might marry. He shows up at my door one day, asks me out, and I say yes. My roommate and I are immediate friends, and she and I will live together until we graduate. Within a few weeks she'll joke that my boyfriend is our third roommate. Pretty soon, he is, more or less.

The campus is glorious. The quad is green and alive, full of sprawling trees, people sunning themselves on the lawn, students moving with purpose as they pass the beautiful old stone buildings that make up the heart of this place. Healy Hall, Copley, Gaston. The portrait of a university from a movie. I walk the paths from one part of campus to the next on my way to class, always full of awe, each new morning a thrill. Sometimes I'm alone, sometimes I'm hand in hand with this boyfriend. He and I immediately become a fixture on campus, we're always together; with his long hair and big smile, he stands out among the other students. I think he is the most beautiful boy I've ever seen.

"I love it here," I tell my mother over the phone each time she calls.

The hallway of my dormitory floor has a single phone booth to share among over fifty students—ancient, wood paneled, with a heavy door framing a glass window. Whenever the phone rings, whoever is nearby answers it, then wanders the halls, yelling out the name of the call's recipient, banging on the doors of people's rooms.

"Donna, it's your mom again!"

People get to know my parents, my mother especially, because she calls so often. When my parents come to visit again, it's like they know my floormates already because they make small talk with everyone who picks up the phone.

The people in my hall stay up late into the night on weekends, weekdays, too; we sit on the floor outside our rooms on the ugly old carpet, talking about life, playing stupid games until we're half asleep. One night we have an epic water fight, something I'll remember for the rest of my life. I can still picture the makeshift barricades. We get in so much trouble with the RAs but it's worth it.

Best of all are my classes. When I applied to college, my parents made me sign up for business school. They want me to be an accountant to take advantage of my math brain, but also because accountants are always needed, much like nurses and teachers. To my mother and father—and my father especially, who didn't go to college—this is the entire point of a university education, to prepare for work that allows you to avoid the hardships they lived through as children of immigrant families. College is meant to help a person find a steady job. So at Georgetown, I start my education as an accounting major, and anyone who knows me today finds this a shock if I tell them.

But thank God for the Jesuits. Because of their focus on the liberal arts, I must fulfill requirements in literature, theology, political science, sociology, psychology, philosophy, and even theater. At first, I don't see the sense in taking courses that seem so irrelevant to my major, but then I start attending them and I am in love. I love every subject I'm taking, all the connections I see between my poli sci and my philosophy classes. Having professors who are also Catholic priests becomes a norm, priests with PhDs who challenge my ideas, who not only survive my doubts about God but push my questions harder, further. I am so surprised to end up in long, lively conversations with Jesuits who take my atheism in stride, who listen with respect and interest to my questions. I've never met priests like this before, I didn't know they existed. The Jesuits sometimes invite students over for dinner or lunch at their residence on campus, and when they invite me, I always say yes. They make me feel welcomed, most of all as a fellow traveler alive with curiosity.

My brain has awoken in ways that will change the course of my future and eventually lead me to pursue a doctorate. Soon, I am thriving, not just socially, but intellectually. I've never been happier.

Then one day I fall. Everything about me collapses. I remember being huddled under the covers of my dormitory bed, I remember the scratchy fabric of the cheap comforter my mother and I bought at Job Lot, a discount store in Rhode Island where you can buy just about anything—a garden hose, dog food, dishes, extra-long twin sheets for college. I remember the orange glow of a nearby lamp, the rest of the room dark.

"I don't know what's wrong with me," I tell my roommate when I can't get out of bed. I tell the same thing to my boyfriend and my parents when they call, worried.

A gnawing darkness has come from nowhere; it grabs my ankle and yanks me down into it. The bright sunlit world of my Georgetown life has broken into pieces; a curtain has fallen to reveal a great nothingness behind it. Think *The Truman Show*, or even *The Matrix*—but I've unwittingly gone behind the veil. I have no interest in taking the red pill, and if someone offered me the blue one and told me I could go back to how I was before, I would do this in a heartbeat.

I don't know how this happens, or what triggers this shift in my body, my brain. It doesn't make sense, nothing makes sense. I have everything I've always wanted, friends, a boyfriend who adores me, the college of my dreams, classes I love, parents who care deeply, a wonderful grandma who sends me notes and magazine subscriptions to my college address. And yet, I am suddenly drowning.

What I do realize quickly is no one can reach me in this pit of darkness where I dwell, no one can see me well enough to pull me out. Nothing moves me, not the sunshine beating down on the quad, not the beautiful boyfriend who chose me out of everyone else, not the voices of my parents on the other end of the phone trying to help from home. What eclipses me is more powerful than regular depression, though if this were happening today, I'm sure I'd immediately be sent into therapy. But back in the early '90s, seeing a therapist wasn't the norm. So I sink and sink while everyone else around me looks on helplessly.

"Sweetheart, did something happen? Something you're not telling us?" my mother asks nearly every day, her worried voice bright through the phone.

"No. Nothing. Everything is the same as it was," I tell her, because it's true and it is.

I am what's different. Something inside me has changed and I can't change it back.

Have you ever gotten stuck in the abyss? I hope not, for your sake. It is an emptiness that nothing can fill, a place where no one can reach you. You can claw and claw at the walls in the blackness but find no purchase.

The first time it happens after I arrive at Georgetown, I am lost, I don't know what to do or how to comprehend it or if there is a cure. I've never been here before so it is the most terrifying experience of affliction I will endure during my adult lifetime. Eventually I come to understand it as part of my makeup, and even though I fear this tendency in myself, I will also learn how to pull myself out after weeks or occasionally months of being stuck there. But this first time is particularly frightening because I do not know if there is any way out, or if I will be here forever. It is a kind of torture. The first time I also have no words, so I can't even explain it to anyone.

Over the years, when I fall into this place again as I am unfortunately prone to do, I know it scares the people around me because it is so total. The people who love me worry I might take my own life. But it's not quite like this, either. The desire to end my life is not a part of it, it's not even nearby. It's the opposite in many ways, because what I experience is a total loss of desire—a loss of will of any kind. A sort of paralysis of personhood.

The abyss is a place where life no longer makes sense. Where nothing makes sense. There is no point to anything, big or small, whether it's going out with a friend or reading a book or doing laundry. It's a loss of not merely meaning but Meaning. Life's reason goes missing and you cannot unearth it again, place it back in your sights. It's like someone knocked it sideways by accident and it's beyond even your peripheral vision.

I learn to be ashamed of this propensity of mine, not because anyone has shamed me for it, but because I don't want to frighten my friends and loved ones, and because I often wonder why other people in my life don't seem to have collapses so total as I do. Maybe they suffer them alone, they tell no one, able to get through it without showing it to the world. But in my case, my whole world comes to a halt and there is no way for me to hide it. I am totally and wholly alone when I am in this place, and because words fail me, it's difficult to make anyone understand.

What if you go get something to eat?
What if you go out with some friends?
What if you go on a trip?

People are always trying to help solve the equation that will provide me a staircase up and out of my darkness, well-meaning and hopeful. But the problem is not caused by something that *happened*, the problem is coming from within.

I have to find a way out on my own.

If my mother is the parent who does her best to turn me into a person of faith, my father is the one who accidentally seeds this darkness into my mind. He has it, too, this propensity to think far too much, so much that during my twenties and thirties, there are days when his whole self falls off a cliff. But during college I don't realize this yet about my father. I haven't witnessed it in him quite so clearly until I'm in graduate school, when tragedy strikes, and I am forced to watch as he plummets. Eventually I will recognize that this thing in him is also in myself, but he and I will never discuss it, not during his lifetime. I won't ever know if he realizes that his suffering is the same as mine. I grow to believe it's in our genes, genes that only he and I share, leaving my mother and my grandmother unscathed by this thing that haunts the both of us.

Looking back, I see the tremendous conflict between what my mother tried to give me and what my father gave me accidentally. My mother worked her whole life to give me faith in God, yet my father passed along the part of me that would cause me to lose sight of God altogether, this pit of darkness inside me. Each of these defining features from my parents—my mother's light, my father's darkness—intermingling in their daughter, canceling each other out. My mother's propensity for belief, for hope, for life beyond death, eclipsed by the abyss within my father that was burned into me from birth, this black hole in my brain that swallows all the light.

Sometimes I wonder if my mother tried so hard to turn me into a person of faith because she could see I was my father's daughter; that I inherited both his math brain and his darkness. Maybe she knew that to survive this inheritance, I would need belief in something beyond the abyss, or I might get stuck in its emptiness forever. Sometimes I can see only the differences between my mother and me, how certain she was of God, so unwavering, how belief simmered underneath her every move, like a secret ingredient, allowing her to enjoy a peace and contentment that eludes so many of us—people like my father and, through him, people like me.

The abyss comes for me.

Eventually I learn about the Dark Night of the Soul, and to appreciate how my intimacy with the abyss is also the thing inside me that keeps me on a never-ending search for Meaning and therefore God. That the thing which turns me into a sick soul also makes me into a person who never stops trying to resolve this conflict. That the philosophy student I am at Georgetown is also the same young woman who—upon her graduation—will go on to get a PhD in Religious Studies, Theology, Spirituality, Mysticism. That as I get older, I will come to appreciate this part of me, at least during the times when I am not wallowing within it and when I can see it from a distance. Because within my propensity to peer into the abyss or worse, tip down into it, also lies my intellect, my insatiable hunger for knowledge, my endless questions about the meaning of life and our existence, the things that make us human. It's the place where I will learn to wait for God, where I will wish for God with all my might, where I will come to believe that it is only God who can possibly break through my darkness and pull me out. That doing so is beyond any human capacity.

But before all this, while I am still at Georgetown, this is the point in my story where my atheism sets in and hardens. As I fall down into the abyss again and again over the course of college, arms flailing yet unable to grab on to any single thing, I am desperately searching for something real and solid, something to break my landing. Something to stop the fall altogether. I wish for God, but God doesn't come. It's not that I think that God is ignoring me; I come to believe that God was never there at all. So I learn to rescue myself because no one else is coming to save me.

My fall semester passes and one day I emerge from the darkness. I have no idea why, I just wake up one morning and I am out. The world has righted itself, the veil over the abyss is back, hiding it, so I can see the world's beauty again, participate in its Meaning. I can take in all the good around me once more. In a way, I guess you could say that it's like being born again.

"I'm feeling so much better," I tell my mother over the pay phone in the dormitory hallway.

"Oh, Donna! I'm so glad to hear that!" Her voice is thrilled but I can tell she is crying. This whole situation has held her in a state of terror. "What happened to make things better?"

"I don't know."

"You don't know? Not even a little?"

"No."

Now she is perplexed. "But *something* had to change, can you think what it might be?"

I shake my head inside the narrow wooden cubicle even though she can't see me, the door shut tight and shielding me from my floormates. "Mom, I really have no idea," I say, because this is the absolute truth. But I understand the urgency in her voice to find an answer to this mystery. Like her, I don't want it to happen again.

"Well, all that matters is you're feeling better," she concedes. "I'm so happy, sweetheart."

"Me too, Mom."

We hang up, my heart is full, the day is full—of possibility, hope, socializing and intellectualizing and hanging out with friends and my boyfriend, who stuck with me through this terrible phase. I wander the campus on my way to classes just like before, like nothing happened, like I didn't experience a collapse of my brain and world so total, there were moments when I was nearly catatonic. I return to the cafeteria and eat all the things I've learned to enjoy amid the bad university food, indulging in giant bowls of sugared cereal, the kind my mother wouldn't allow in the house when I was growing up. Everyone around me is relieved. My boyfriend, my roommate, my new friends in college. Life returns to normal again. Almost.

11

Thank you, Sartre.

One day during my second semester of college, a hand reaches out to me through the black—the hand of Sartre, crossing time and space and death. This is how I come to think of it. It happens in my Intro to Philosophy class. We've read *No Exit*, and the professor teaches us about Bad Faith, and the existentialist concept of anxiety. I recognize myself in all we discuss. I feel like I've been found.

I remember this day so clearly. I can see everything around me. The classroom full of long narrow wooden tables, row after row, with five, maybe six chairs behind each one. I am sitting in the front, maybe two students from the end. There is the bright glow of the overhead lights, the professor at the front of the class with his thick, dark-rimmed glasses.

If I had believed in God back then, I would have thanked God for Sartre repeatedly.

Over the course of my first year at Georgetown, I experience a kind of conversion to philosophy, one which solidifies that same spring. I was so resistant to taking courses in philosophy initially, because they have nothing to do with being an accounting major. But as the year progresses, I start to look forward to philosophy, I am seeing parallels in the ideas I'm studying for my other classes, and this makes my brain happy. But on that first day of Sartre, I cease being a divided self and I become a believer.

As we discuss existentialism, I learn of the abyss, as well as notions of being and nothingness. Finally—*finally*—I find the words to describe what it is that I've been suffering. I come to understand my crisis as existential in nature, that it's a crisis of being, that there are other people who suffer it, too. I am not unique, not alone after all, there are entire areas of philosophical thought devoted to describing, understanding, and surviving this affliction. Reading philosophy is all I want to do from here on out, philosophy becomes the therapist I need but do not have in real life. I learn to seek my therapy on the page—from Sartre, Camus, Nietzsche, and eventually Heidegger. A mirror has been held up to my insides, and I can finally see who I really am.

The relief is enormous.

I call my parents on the pay phone in the hallway. "I want to major in philosophy."

"But what would you do with it?" my mother asks.

I am afraid to tell my parents the truth behind my desire. They want what happened to me to be a thing of the past, something we stick in a back drawer that is never discussed again. "I just really like it," is all I say.

"No, you are there to study accounting," my father insists.

"Okay," I agree, but only because I know the Jesuits' plan, which is to essentially force me to take more philosophy until my sophomore year and even beyond.

My father wants to make sure I understand that I did not come to Georgetown to do something so impractical, lest I end up living back at my parents' house after graduation. "There are no jobs for philosophers," he asserts.

"I know," I agree, but I don't. Or at least, I don't care.

I am already planning my spring semester.

The study of philosophy *is* practical for me. The most practical thing I can do for myself at the time. Studying it changes my whole life, in ways I look back on and see as essential to my identity, to all that I become in my future, but also to my salvation from this darkness that lives inside of me, that rears up and takes over my whole brain for a while, paralyzing me. After that first experience of the abyss, my insides are scarred. I want to understand this gaping hole within, learn how to fill it, kick some dirt over it and pat it down until it's firm and solid. Or at least, I want to learn how to live with whatever this is that my brain does that scares me and everyone else. In a perfect world, what I search for in the philosophical tomes that begin to fill my growing college library is a cure.

At Georgetown, I both thrive and struggle to the point of collapse. Mainly I thrive. In my studies, the best part of me has awakened and taken over my heart, my soul, my body. My brain is more alive than ever and I fall in love with everything I read. In the philosophy department, I find the professor-mentors who will be with me for the rest of my life, even now decades later, who offer me the books that drag me up and out of the darkness, who help me see an intellectual future I never could have dreamed of before Georgetown.

One concept becomes my obsession, an idea I return to again and again over the course of my life and all the trials I'll face within it:

Sartre's idea of Bad Faith.

Imagine you are a dancer, your whole life revolves around your ability to leap and *balancé*. Dance is all you know and care for, you cannot imagine your life without it. In fact, you feel your life would be over if you were not a dancer. It becomes your profession, you can't pay your rent without it, your happiness depends on it. One day on your way to ballet class, you are in a horrible car accident. Your leg is crushed, the doctors amputate it. Afterward, your world collapses. *You* collapse, you implode, you no longer know how to make your way in the world, you care nothing for the world and anyone in it if you cannot dance. Your ability to make sense of your place within humanity and all existence has vanished. There is no meaning unless dance is a part of your life, unless you, yourself, are a dancer. Your life is pointless, you cannot go on. You lose the will to live.

For Sartre, it is dangerous to allow our worlds to rest entirely on something that can be gone at any moment, something temporary, contingent, that depends on fate and chance (say, our limbs, or say, a person, a spouse, our children). When we refuse to see that the roles we have come to occupy—dancer, lover, mother, surgeon, best friend, etc.—can disappear in an instant, with an accident, a tragedy, a tiny shift in the fabric of the universe, we are living in Bad Faith. Everything we do and love and are, is contingent. Our loved ones can be lost, our bodies and their parts can cease to function, our professions can go *poof* overnight. For Sartre, to build our existence, our Meaning, upon the foundation of the contingent is a recipe for disaster. It's exactly what will make us vulnerable to a plunge into the abyss that we may never crawl out of, stuck as we will be in the prison of the nothing for all eternity. If this sounds a lot like hell, for Sartre it *is*.

So how does one manage *not* to live in Bad Faith?

By an embrace of this nothing, the abyss, the truth of it. To live in the face of our reality that everything is contingent, with a constant awareness of the temporal nature of all things; for Sartre we cannot and should not, say, root our meaning and purpose in our own children, in our roles as mothers or fathers, because this can be catastrophic. Every role we occupy—wife, sister, daughter, banker, cook, teacher—can disappear in seconds, and with it our whole sense of our place in the world and our purpose.

I learned this truth because of the college boyfriend I loved. The first time we broke up, my whole heart fell to pieces. I plunged into the depths of despair, though now I had a name for how I'd been living: Bad Faith. I'd hung my happiness on the love of a person who could wake up one morning and decide we were over. Which also meant my happiness vanished the second he was gone. I'd been a fool to pretend that he would be with me forever.

But of course, we do this all the time, right? We must build our lives on *something*, and usually our building blocks rest on love of the very contingent humans who orbit our world, family and friends who make life good and beautiful and worthwhile. We build our lives on our professions, too, on meaningful work if we are lucky enough to find it. All things which can disappear nearly instantly, throwing us into a tailspin.

Of course, whereas Sartre's answer to the predicament of our humanity involves a willingness to see beyond the veil of contingency to the nothingness behind it, to accept that on the other side of every single thing that brings us joy and meaning is utter isolation, Christianity has a different answer: God and Jesus and faith. For Christians, there isn't a nothingness undergirding all things, there is a *somethingness* that is beautiful and good and true and eternal. If we are believers, God and Jesus are meant to be the cushion that stops us from an eternal plummet into the abyss, from dwelling in this hell on earth forever, the arms that cradle us and carry us through the darkness until we are ready to stand by ourselves again.

This is where the difference between a believing Christian and a faith-challenged person like me reveals itself. I plunge into that darkness and wish for someone to carry me to the other side of this hell. But the only way I ever get there is if I somehow find the path out again alone. It's an awful way to be. So during college, my brain's potential to plunge into this nothingness gnawed through my heart and soul like a terminal disease. I never wanted it to happen again, so I began to live my life toward the hope of preventing it at all costs.

If God and Jesus weren't coming to save me, I'd have to find another route toward my own salvation. I read all I could of existentialism and set out never to live in Bad Faith. I would approach my life as Sartre prescribed it, with a sense that the abyss was just on the other side of everything I was and did, everything I cared about and loved. I soon learned this was an impossibly lonely way to be. Try as I might to keep it up, I could exist for only so long before I was living in Bad Faith yet again. I may have entered college as a precocious atheist, but thanks to Sartre, I soon became a fundamentalist one.

12

An interlude about the reformation, the difference between Catholics and Protestants, and fears of excommunication.

I am going to tell you something that will be difficult to believe if you are evangelical: During college as I plunged into the abyss and endured one Dark Night of the Soul after another, not a single person in my very Catholic existence thought to hand me a Bible. Not a Jesuit priest, not even my mother. It's also true that if they had, I probably wouldn't have cracked it open. After all, why would I? It wasn't something I'd learned to consult or understand, and if I'd tried to read it, I probably would've gotten lost in all its many books anyway.

For those of you who didn't already know this about Catholics, let me be the one to tell you: Catholics don't read the Bible. Not like Protestants do, and definitely not like evangelical Protestants do. We don't *know* the Bible, we don't learn it, we don't learn to *use* it. When I was a child, my father may have read to me all the time from my children's Bible, but once I got older and after I'd memorized all the appealing kid stories about floods and animals, serpents and forbidden apples, David and Goliath, Samson, Delilah, and that devious haircut, I didn't think about it much anymore. I certainly didn't actually touch a Bible over the course of my Catholic education. Most Catholics don't, or at least, the ones from my generation didn't.

To give you an idea of how deep our Bible avoidance goes: I have a PhD in Religion from the Catholic University of America, and throughout my entire doctorate, only one course related to the Bible was required. And remember when I told you about my Confirmation classes during high school? We didn't study the Bible during those evening sessions when I was so bored I thought I might disintegrate into the ether. We studied the official catechism of the Catholic Church. The catechism is the instruction book for what Catholics are supposed to believe and it's written by the pope and his advisors. It's as fat as the Bible itself but it is not the Bible itself. Catholics—at least if they are Catholics like me, growing up in a devout household like mine—go to CCD classes. CCD stands for Confraternity of Christian Doctrine, which is just a fancy way of labeling catechism classes, where we all learn what the pope and his fellow VIP Catholic officials want us to. I don't even remember having a Bible during the entirety of my young adult life, aside from the picture-book one with Jesus and the lions on its cover, which sat for years untouched on our living room bookshelves once I became too old for it.

To be Catholic, no Bible is necessary! That could be the tradition's tagline.

To many of you reading this, I know this must sound like heresy.

Well, speaking of heresy, this is also the juncture where the Protestant Reformation becomes as real as it gets, where it divides us Catholics from everyone else like Moses parting the sea, only to leave the Catholics behind on the shore. All those squabbles back during the time of Martin Luther about access to the Bible, who gets to read it and who doesn't, who gets to be in charge of what it means, come to define the true difference between a Catholic and a Protestant.

Protestants actually pick up the Bible, read it, and believe it is their God-given responsibility to understand it for themselves, that they have the authority to interpret each passage, each story, each verse that they read on their own. This is also why so many evangelical college students and hip twenty-somethings are already budding pastors and church leaders practically from the time they are teenagers. Yet finding a Catholic priest under the age of thirty pretty much requires a worldwide manhunt at this juncture of history. If a Catholic comes to believe they might have a teensy bit of authority over this faith and should share it with others, it's a bona fide miracle.

Growing up and throughout our lifetimes, we Catholics learn to be passive when it comes to understanding our faith. We are raised to be listeners, meant to imbibe more than to understand, meant to be obedient to whatever we are told by the hierarchy of the Church. The Bible? It's the domain of that hierarchy—the pope, the College of Cardinals, the College of Bishops, all the way on down to the priests. *They* are the ones who read the Bible and take charge of it, it's *their* job to tell us about the stories and teachings and meanings in their own words and according to how they've decided to interpret all of this.

We Catholics let *them* read the Bible *for us*. The hierarchy and its priests are the *filters* through which we hear the Bible stories according to their beliefs about what's in there and what it tells us.

During the Reformation, the Catholic Church and its officials fought hard against the printing press and its ability to mass-produce the Bible because they believed that handing out Bibles to every man, woman, and child was dangerous business. If everybody could read scripture and decide what it meant for themselves, then church officials might lose control of the Word and how they wielded it to keep everybody in line. The hierarchy and its priests might very well lose the plot and us believers in the process. Direct access to the Bible was so dangerous, according to them, that a great schism across Christendom was a better option for the Catholic hierarchy than giving in and letting us all study it for ourselves.

This is still pretty much the way things operate.

We Catholics go to church and sit there like stones, listening to the priests tell us what to think about the Bible—this is literally what we do. The vast majority of us let the priests inform us as to what the Bible says and tell us what it means, then we go home and eat a really big lunch until we are sleepy and ready for a nap. It rarely occurs to any of us to pick up that Bible on our own time. I'm generalizing here about Catholics, of course, and there are plenty who read the Bible regularly, and there are Catholic PhDs who specialize in New Testament, among other biblically related subjects. But I'll tell you two other stories to illustrate what I mean, to try and make it sink in for all you evangelical folk who have come to this table. Before I do, I'll remind you one more time that I managed to get a PhD while almost never picking up a Bible more than once in a single semester. I also graduated from Georgetown University, which is both Catholic and Jesuit, and I never picked one up there, either. Not once. Yes, this is the truth.

Story 1

"But this book isn't *Christian*," a nice young woman sitting in my New York City apartment is politely telling me.

I am nearly out of graduate school and I'm in the process of co-writing my first book with one of my closest friends, also a Catholic theologian. Our book is about dating and spirituality (no, not at all like *I Kissed Dating Goodbye*). We've given a draft of it to some college students, all evangelical, who came to us by way of an evangelical colleague. There are five, maybe six young men and women sitting on my worn-out university-issue couches and chairs alongside Jason, my cowriter. The whole lot of them apparently agree with what this woman has just observed about our book.

"What do you mean, it's not Christian?" I ask.

"It's not Bible-based," another person in the group says.

"Um, so?" My eyebrows arch. "I'm still not understanding."

One of the young men opens to a chapter where Jason has written about Thomas Aquinas. "See here, this argument is based in Aquinas."

Jason is nodding.

I am nodding along with him. "And that's a problem because...?"

The young woman who'd spoken up originally is still trying to put it to us as nicely as she can. "You've based this in Catholic theology, not the Bible, so it's not really Christian."

Honestly, people—and I am telling you the truth here—I'm still not understanding what she's going on about, or why the entire group keeps bringing up the Bible and the conspicuous absence of Bible verses in our book—conspicuous for them, not even a blip to us. Jason and I have more theology in this draft of the manuscript than any reasonable person out on the dating scene really needs to think about. And yet there it is—the problem these students have identified for us. There is a good deal of Thomas Aquinas and Bernard Lonergan, courtesy of Jason, a whole lot of Dorothy Day, Julian of Norwich, and a bunch of contemporary feminist theologians, courtesy of me. For us, this book is already, like, super theological. So why are they worrying so much about the Bible?

Eventually the nice young Christians say good-bye, we thank them, they leave my apartment, and Jason and I look at each another. *Huh? What do you make of that?* Somewhere in the middle of us processing what they told us, a lightbulb goes on in my brain, bright and glowing.

Ohhhhhhhhhhhhh.

I may have escaped graduate school with cracking the Bible in only a single class, but I did study history while there and I learned about Martin Luther and his aftermath. So this is the moment I finally grasp that these nice evangelical students' interest in the Bible, and our own shrugs about its relative absence in our book, is an actual representation of the results of the Protestant Reformation. Evidence of it is right there on the pages of that draft we wrote. To be Catholic is to read and prize the likes of Julian of Norwich and Thomas Aquinas and to use theologians and their theology to base an argument of how to live a life, how to make ethical decisions, how to determine what is good and what is not. To be evangelical Christian, to be Protestant, is to read the Bible in order to do all of the above.

Point made and understood.

But Jason and I didn't revise the book accordingly. To us, theology was why we'd come to write it in the first place, and where we'd happily remain. We're Catholics, after all.

Story 2

My second story about the very real effects of the Protestant Reformation on Catholics comes a few years later. By now I've had my PhD awhile and I am visiting yet another Catholic, Jesuit college to talk to students who've read my more recent book, *Sex and the Soul*, about sex and faith on campus. A professor invited me to do a Q&A with his students who have read it.

One of the main arguments of the book and findings from my national study is that as far as beliefs and practices around sex go,

Catholic students at Catholic colleges may as well be secular. Their faith tradition has virtually no bearing on their attitudes about sex, and most of them have learned to divorce being Catholic from their beliefs about sex. This is due to the general absence of practical literature, conversation, and teaching for Catholic young adults with respect to sex and relationships, and the fact that most guidance coming down from the hierarchy to young adult Catholics is simply one big *no* to sex, and this is from a bunch of aging, celibate men.

But the students in this undergraduate Catholic theology class have about a million ideas on what the tradition could offer their sex and dating lives, and we have a vibrant conversation about their views and proposals toward this end. So I suggest to a young woman she should write an article about dating and theology.

Exactly here is where the divide between Protestant and Catholic rears up its head again—but this time I see it clearly. This time, I can't not see it. My national study included evangelical colleges and they, too, are reading my book and inviting me to campus to talk about the findings of my research. So by now I've spent tons of time with evangelical people, young and old, and I know all about the authority evangelical youth feel they have to speak on matters of faith—the exact kind of authority Catholics *don't* feel. Like, it's absent from us, a missing gene left out of our makeup.

I go on to explain to these nice Catholic college students in this theology class that within young adult, evangelical circles, all kinds of people are writing books about dating and relationships, yet it dismays me that in the Catholic tradition, there are none. That this young woman with her big theological ideas should consider writing a book herself so the Catholic young adults could catch up a bit.

The young woman is shaking her head. "But if I wrote something, I'd get excommunicated."

"No you wouldn't," I counter.

"Yes, I would," she counters back.

"But why?" I ask.

Her reasons? She cannot make a public argument about sex, dating, and her faith, because she has no authority and no forum for offering her ideas. She is not a member of the Catholic hierarchy, she is not a priest, and her ideas challenge the virtually useless and nearly nonexistent wisdom about sex and young adulthood already offered by official Catholic teaching. She is just an ordinary person, an ordinary Catholic, and ordinary Catholics have no right to speak on such matters, she believes. This is not the first time I've heard this business about the potential for excommunication from a young adult Catholic. It's something I end up hearing a lot as I encourage Catholic college students to share their visions and ideas for how Catholicism might better inform their lives and decision making because this is desperately needed among Catholic youth, especially on the topics of sex, dating, and relationships.

I explain this to the young woman before me—as I do to others like her—that she not only has the *right* but the *responsibility* to herself and her peers to try and speak on matters related to Catholic morality and faith. But she still does not believe me *because she is not a priest nor is she a celibate Catholic official in any way.* So to her the choice is as follows: either remain silent or get excommunicated for speaking out. And she is not being facetious.

Hello again, you Protestant Reformation you.

Somehow, through osmosis, Sunday masses, CCD classes, and Catholic schooling, and perhaps in the ventilation systems of the churches we Catholics attend as we grow up, a belief takes shape within us that we have no right to speak up about our feelings and ideas in the areas that Catholic morality touches us. Only priests and bishops, cardinals and popes have that right. We can read and think and form opinions all we want, but unlike the evangelical who reads the Bible, has an insight, and say, plants a church because of this, then installs himself as pastor (because let's face it, usually it's a guy, unless you're Nadia Bolz-Weber), Catholic youth are typically completely disempowered within our faith tradition. I mean, I know

I was. Catholics in general are disempowered. The muscle that is faith, the passion we may have had for it as children, tends to atrophy as we grow up and leave the house. The result of years of sitting back and listening in the pews and being taught that it's the role of the priest to do all of this for us and that, really, all we can do is all we've already been doing: sit there and listen, sit there and be obedient. So most of us learn to stay quiet, to stop caring overly much, to not use our voices toward the end of parsing out our faith in relation to morality and beliefs, to how we make our choices and live our actual lives. This is the prevailing wisdom, at least.

Anything more might get us kicked out.

So, as a college student when I am desperately flailing around and trying to find something, anything, to pull me out of this terrible, senseless place of nothingness that keeps tripping up my whole existence, it is Camus and Simone de Beauvoir and Sartre and Heidegger and eventually Hegel who will form the very human parade that leads me up and out of that abysmal pit and into the living, breathing world again and again over the years. They are the gods of my salvation during this time in my life. They are the hope that shows up for me when I need it and when God—and the Bible and everyone in it for that matter—is nowhere to be found.

13

Here comes Santa Claus.

I am twenty-one. I've come back to the house I share with my college roommates to a message from my mother on our answering machine.

Hi, sweetheart, it's Mom! I just wanted to see how you were doing. I also wanted to know how your test went. I've been praying for you all day, and God has given you so many gifts! Okay, sweetheart, call me back! I love you!

My college roommates love listening to my mother's messages. The group of us live half a block from M Street, the main drag of Georgetown, and around the corner from Booeymonger, a sandwich shop as much a staple for Georgetown students as eating and drinking at The Tombs near campus. We also live dangerously close to a place called Quick Pita, which is open all night and where everyone lines up at 3:00 a.m. to order their steak and cheese sandwiches on the way home from the bars and parties. My roommates and I do our best to create rules to curb our Quick Pita and Booeymonger habits, especially the Quick Pita visits, which we inevitably regret the following morning. At one point there is a sheet hanging on the back of our front door listing house chores, the rule being that whoever succumbs to the middle of the night siren call of Quick Pita must be the next person to vacuum the living room or clean the kitchen.

It is common for me to arrive home after class or from my work-study job to an enthusiastic message on the answering machine like the one above from my mother. She is always calling to check in, to see how I'm doing, because I am her only child and she keeps track of what I tell her, eager to ask how this or that went. Without fail, she talks of God and prayer straight into the machine.

Sometimes my roommates save my mother's messages to play them back for visitors to our house. The reason is not the God talk, but because of my mother's accent. It is beyond strong, unmistakably Rhode Island. So very Rhode Island that when I was a child and learning about silent vowels and consonants in school, I concluded there must be a silent r. The notion of the silent r arrived like an *aha* for me, and I wondered when I'd be taught about it in school. I kept trying to figure out why *car* was spelled c-a-r because when my parents spoke the word, it came out CAAH. Same with park, which they pronounced PAAHK. Think Matt Damon and Ben Affleck in *Good Will Hunting* but with even more flare. When the reading lesson about the silent r never arrived, it bothered me so much, I asked my mother about it and she laughed.

"There isn't a silent r, sweetheart," she said. Then she explained to me about accents.

So my college roommates thoroughly enjoy saving my mother's messages because instead of beginning with general greetings like, *How are you?* as their own parents did, pronunciations careful and clear, my mother is prone to a cheerful "Ha ya dooin', sweethaaht?" My mother's personality is as large as can be—voice replete with emotion, laughter, joy, her accent a technicolor dream coat she wears over it with pride. Tony Soprano but ladylike and full of light, hope, happiness.

Two of my roommates and I have lived together since our first year at Georgetown, and one will become my lifelong friend, the irreplaceable kind, who many years later will strap her newborn to her chest and make the journey across Brooklyn to my apartment a few hours after my husband leaves me. She will arrive, baby snuggled into her, and the first thing she will do is change my sheets, then look at me and say, "There, your bed is like new." But that is still many years away.

Now we are still in college, not long from graduating, not far from the afternoon when she and I, along with our third roommate, will take one of our favorite photos from that time in our lives: two of us in a supermarket shopping cart, long legs dangling over the sides, the third person leaning over the handlebar, all of us laughing like we are having the time of our lives because we are, and we've been driving that cart all over the neighborhood of Georgetown. We're not the ones who steal it, someone else does, we never know who, but we find it stranded in the middle of the lovely, cobbled streets and hijack it from there. That photo never fails to remind me that life is good and beautiful and fun and silly sometimes. A reminder I sometimes need.

On this day, when I walk through the front door into the living room of the house I share with my roommates and hear my mother's latest cheerful greetings, I groan. Then I call her back.

"Hi, sweetheart!" she greets me, like always.

I start in immediately with what annoys me. "Mahhmmm."

"What, sweetheart?"

"Why do you have to always attribute everything I am to God."

"God has given you many gifts!"

"I hate when you do this," I tell her, because I do. I resent it. I resent all that it implies. "Can't you just once acknowledge that maybe *I* am the one who did well on a test, or that it's because of something about *me* that I do well in school? Can it *not* be because you prayed to God that something good happened in my life?"

"But, sweetheart, there is nothing wrong with praying for you, and besides, prayer works. And it's wonderful that God gave you gifts and that you *use* those gifts. Even if you don't realize that you are doing it. Some people don't use the gifts that God gives them. But you are using those amazing gifts and I see you doing this."

"Mom!"

My mother sighs. She knows my hands are figuratively over my ears, that they are perpetually closing off my ability to hear such things, that they have been doing this for many years by this point. "I love you very much, sweetheart," she says.

"I love you, too," I tell her.

We hang up. The cycle of this conversation repeats day after day, week after week.

My mother prays for me and lets me know it. I tell her what I've done or what's gone well in my life and school, and she attributes it to her praying and God answering. I get really annoyed. There are two things going on under the surface between us.

First, I resent the idea that my achievements are not my own. I resent that my mother is always chalking up anything I've done, everything I am that is good, to someone else. This God person that I don't believe in. Like she is always pulling the things I'm proud of out of my own grasp, saying they're not mine to have and embody, but the work of somebody else, someone I can't see and who definitely feels absent from my life. When I convey this to her, she is always ready with an answer that goes something like this, and which makes me grumble:

"What's so awful about God giving you gifts, sweetheart?"

The other problem is that throughout college I have been tumbling down into this pit of despair like I've said, and swimming in an existential loneliness that is difficult for the people around me to grasp. And while I may not have told my mother this at the time, I'll tell you this now: When I am there in that darkness, I wish for *any-thing* to come and pull me out. If God decided to show up with a pulley and some rope, I would grab on happily to let God yank me back up. But I am there in that pit often, and God is nowhere to be found. The more I have to rescue myself, the more I resent God's absence from my life during all those dark nights of my soul. So whenever my mother starts on with her talk of prayer and God answering these prayers that apparently allow me to do well in school or have a good week or whatever she is praying about at the time, it makes me angry.

As I look back on this time in my life when I was surrounded constantly by so much God-talk, I realize that what I really and truly felt was abandoned. Why did God bother with everyone else around me but not also me? As far as I was concerned, God couldn't see me at all, didn't even try to, and if I waited around for God to show up and help me out of that darkness, I would still be there wallowing now. So sometimes, when I was on the phone with my poor, well-meaning mother and she was talking about prayer yet again, and I didn't have it in my heart to humor her like I sometimes tried to do, I got mad at her and at God. And I let her know I was mad at both of them.

"Your God is nothing but another Santa Claus," I told her, more than once.

"Sweetheart! Don't say that."

"It's true. You're kidding yourself, Mom. God isn't real. God was never real. God is just some made-up figure people invent to help themselves feel better about life's disappointments and death."

I know. Dear reader, I know. I am being so harsh. I am being awful.

If I could go back and undo those God-is-Santa-Claus conversations with my mother on the phone, or in person when I went home for break, or in the car when we were headed out for pizza or to the supermarket, I would do it in a second. I would ask my mother a whole different set of questions instead. Like:

What does it *feel* like when God answers one of your prayers, Mom?

Do you actually experience God's presence, and what's that like?

Have you ever heard God's voice, and if so, what does it sound like?

Who do you think God is, Mom?

Why do you think God doesn't show up for me?

Am I listening wrong?

Did I do something unforgivable?

Is there something fundamentally missing in me, which makes me unworthy?

Do you think God will ever turn my way?

Is it all just a matter of waiting, Mom?

Do you think I'll be waiting forever?

What's the difference between you and me, Mom—do you know?

But I didn't do this. Not once. Not any of it. And now I can't because she's gone.

Throughout my philosophizing during Georgetown, my intellectual rigor, the way I learn to interrogate the depths of my own mind, it never occurrs to me that right on the other side of such fervent unbelief lie the waters of faith. That the two might be connected. This was exactly St. Augustine's problem, wasn't it, when he was young and struggling himself?

The reason the ideas of Nietzsche and Sartre and their existentialist fellows resonate so deeply in my heart is because we are all struggling with the same things, the proximity of a terrible loneliness, an existentialist angst that also struck the hearts of the likes of St. John of the Cross and Teresa of Ávila, both of whom I will read not long from now in graduate school; that the Dark Night of the Soul is as common an affliction among the most champion of believers as it is among atheists. That doubt has always plagued the most faithful, the mystics who will eventually fascinate me when I go to get my doctorate. That this is all part of their journey, too, it's just that they use different words to describe it, and what they see beyond it has a different outcome. That often on the other side of the long Dark Night is the finding of God.

The terrible irony of this ongoing back and forth with my mother on the subject of prayer and God while I am still in college is that there I am, resisting my mother's claims about the authorship of my actions, my achievements, my successes—resisting like it is the devil himself putting such thoughts and words into my mother's mouth—and meanwhile in my philosophy major I am on a massive search for Meaning with a capital M. I am deeply invested in the notion that there is something greater than myself, but I don't want to call it God. In this search, I am doing things like investigating the relationship between words, *literally in the gap between words*, and how they construct meaning as possible evidence of this. I am reading and theorizing about the love between humans, about any and all relationships between us, even about the ways we connect with people who are no longer alive through the reading of books, our direct lines to people from history.

Such things are my possible miracles, though I would never have used that word, and certainly not in the presence of my mother. But I am obsessed with these possibilities, always and constantly reading and writing about them for my philosophy classes. So over the course of my years at Georgetown, as my brain and intellect come alive, I use my fervor to tear down the faith my mother is trying so hard to give me. And with my fancy Georgetown education, I get better and better at this task. Cleverer, more zealous, smarter, and fiercer about it.

And I am so blind. To my mother, especially, and all the wisdom she holds, that she will offer on a regular basis in the upbeat content of her messages on our answering machine. I am in a sea of riches at Georgetown, going to class among the wealthy, well-traveled children who attended Exeter and Andover for high school, prep schools that cost more than it does to attend Georgetown, whose parents are the heads of giant international corporations. I am quite literally going to class among princes and drinking beer on weekends with the sons of heads of state. I also have plenty of peers whose parents count as wealthy, just not shockingly so, and even others who probably fall on the scale of middle class. But truly the only other person I meet at Georgetown whose parents count as working class like mine is the roommate who becomes that lifelong best friend.

So the other part of the story that is my mother and I during my college years is this: The moment I enter Georgetown, I learn to be ashamed of my parents' humble lives, their working-class stature, their accents, which so clearly betray this background. I learn to be ashamed of my mother's blatant, obvious faith, especially when I see it splashed garishly against the quiet reserve of the faith of others around me, and especially if those others are the wealthy, accomplished parents of friends.

Now, as an adult who can see how lucky I was to have the parents I did, to be given the gift of such unconditional love, I cringe at how I acted back then toward these people who loved me so dearly. At how I began to reject my parents as models for my future and my own career. That I became a person who told her mother she believed in Santa Claus. I loathe how I dismissed her simple wisdom, her fervent belief. Especially given the fact that she—though hurt, I am sure, by the things I said and threw at her with my lofty words and banal ones, too—always took heart and tried again, embarked on yet another new tack with me on the God and prayer front. She never gave up. Never ever.

Today, I can see so clearly that in all those messages she left on our answering machine, my mother was offering a possible answer to my philosophical journey and search, an alternative way out of the abyss I kept falling into, albeit by using words and language I'd concluded were problematic. Finally, in hindsight, I can read between the lines of what she said. And if I could rewrite what I heard on that ridiculous, old-school answering machine that broadcast my mother's voice to everyone in our house, it might go something like this:

Hi, sweetheart, it's Mom! All day I have been engaging in conversation with something that lies beyond myself, I have been wading into the waters of Meaning because I am constantly Connecting with the Beyond, and I am doing so with you in mind, sweetheart. I see the root of all your talents and gifts as beautiful signs that your father and I made you, yes, but also as rooted in something bigger and greater than just us and yourself. What a wonder that in your own life you have learned to tap into such Magnificence, in order to become who you are and to try and figure out how to live a life that is good and worthwhile. I am so proud that you would open yourself to such things by studying, and searching, and asking Big Questions in your philosophy major. How exciting. Okay, call me back, sweetheart! But not too late because you know I go to bed early! Your mother loves you so much!

14

The bridge of darkness.

One night, I am going out. On my way, I have to head down to M Street, in Georgetown's shopping district. I follow M toward Dupont Circle, the next neighborhood over. Maybe I am headed to meet a friend somewhere, or maybe I am headed to a bookstore to pick something up, I don't remember the reason for the trip. All I know is that it's dark out, it's cold, and I am alone.

There's a part of M street where it crosses Rock Creek Park, which is enormous and stretches all the way toward the northern boundaries of DC. At the other end, it reaches the Potomac River, near the Kennedy Center. I often jog in this park during the day, and sometimes follow it into the National Zoo. One of the great benefits of living in DC is that the museums and zoos are free. This is how I become a person who regularly enters the Hirshhorn Museum to see a single, favorite painting, and who often wanders the National Gallery of Art on the Mall.

On this particular trip across Rock Creek, on the very short bridge above it, spanning only a block of M, I halt. I am suddenly dizzy, nauseous, swimming with terrible vertigo. My hands are on the slotted stone wall that lines the street over the park, the many trees reaching up and over it from below, wind rustling the leaves. I don't know if the streetlights are out in this moment, or if there are usually any streetlights there at all, but in my memory this one block is a spot of atypical darkness. While I stand there in the night on the bridge, no one else is crossing it, only me.

I am terrified.

Not because of the lack of light, or the fact that I am alone on this bridge in the dark of the city, but because a pit of emptiness once again opens inside me. I have never been more aware of my aloneness in the world than I am on this bridge in this moment. This is the time before cell phones, so there is no one I can call. I know in my heart that I will always be this way—totally and completely alone. There is nothing and no one who can change this about myself. I can't see a way out, I don't believe there is one. I joke sometimes with my friends about needing a lobotomy, and right now, the thought is not a joke, but an honest wish. I would do anything to relieve myself of this pain and isolation. The existentialist angst is so acute, so total, and I know by now there is no escape. No cure for what I am.

So I stand there paralyzed in the dark of the abyss and the dark above Rock Creek Park on this stretch of M. I stay there a long time, unable to move my body. Maybe other people pass me as I press my hands onto the cold stone wall, but I don't remember seeing any. All these years later, I can still feel the chill wind on my face, hear the rustle of the leaves, see the darkness broken only by the glow of light behind me from the stores at the other end of M.

Eventually I do move, since obviously I didn't stay there forever. I go on my way somehow, though I don't remember which way it was—if I turned back to head home, abandoning the plans that took me toward Dupont, or if I forged ahead toward my destination. And I have no idea how I come up with the will to take one step, then another, finally moving myself across that bridge and out of all that darkness. All I know is that I do and I did.

By the time I am nearing my graduation from Georgetown, I've learned to think of my life as a kind of Jenga tower. All it takes is for one single brick to be removed and everything comes tumbling down. The problem is, I often don't know which brick will topple the tower that is me. Sometimes I can identify it, I can anticipate it and try to fight it off—a breakup with my off-and-on-again boyfriend will do it, for example. In my weakest moments, I use the love I feel for him to build a wall between myself and the abyss, to live for a blissful while in Bad Faith, only to find that when he's no longer there to block the darkness, once again I am standing at the edge of that pit and can see nothing else but a bottomless emptiness. It is not just heartbreak I experience, either, it is something far more frightening and empty. But more often than not, the tip downward seems random—I am walking down M Street, ho hum, on my way somewhere benign, and suddenly it strikes and I am there again, peering into that gaping hole of nothingness.

My attempt to understand why I am this way and what exactly causes the world to tilt begins to form the foundation of my whole life, my world, even my future. To try and understand the nothingness inside me and in the middle of it, to try and find *something*. Because I want to survive. I want to heal this wound somehow, so that my future looks different than what I am enduring at present. By now it no longer occurs to me to hope for God in the black of my despair because I have lost that hope completely. By now I know that God is not coming—that no one is.

During my last year of college, I enroll in a favorite professor's seminar on Heidegger's *Being and Time*. It's a class full of graduate students getting their PhDs in philosophy. I let the professor convince
me I am up to the task, but already in my first week I am drowning.
I show up in his office one day and sit down in the visitor's chair for
students next to his desk.

"I'm going to drop the class," I tell him.

He shakes his head. "No—don't. You can do this, Donna. Keep at
it, and one day you'll get the hang of what Heidegger is saying and
realize you can read him. It's worth the effort, I promise."

I agree, but reluctantly. Reading a single page of Heidegger's
giant, heavy tome takes me a good ten minutes. Reading a few pages
takes forever. But I do it, day in and day out, diligently. I feel lost,
frustrated, like I will never come out the other side of what seems
like Heidegger's gibberish, the way he just makes up terms and uses
them all over the place—terms that are extremely complex to define
and understand. Terms that feel beyond even my very philosophi-
cally minded brain. It's like having to learn another language.

But it turns out my professor is right.

One day, I open Heidegger and suddenly I understand. It's like
the sun comes out over my world. I am soon in love with reading
him, with the way he is always reaching past the limits of language
to invent new terms to capture a concept for which we simply don't
yet have the words. Reading Heidegger *is* like learning a new language and I adore it. I come to think of him as a poet-philosopher.
My Heidegger seminar becomes my favorite class. Several of his
concepts hold me rapt and I obsess over them, searching for metaphors and everyday experiences to illuminate them further:
ready-to-hand and *present-at-hand* become the most important ones
for me.

For Heidegger, most things are ready-to-hand for us, so much that they become rote, we don't have to think of them, we just use them effortlessly.

The classic example is a door. We go through doors all the time, we don't have to think about doors to use them, it's just automatic. Doors are typically not present-at-hand. Sure, occasionally we need to read a sign on a door that tells us to *push* or *pull*, but then once we read it, we're good, and we go through. We barely notice doors otherwise.

But once in a while, something on the door breaks—the knob, a lock, the handle, and the door stops working, it becomes stuck, we can't seem to get through it, it must be fixed. We suddenly must become *aware* of this thing we normally don't think about, that we usually contend with as though it's invisible. This is when the door becomes present-at-hand.

For Heidegger, something is present-at-hand when we are forced to contemplate its existence, when we are *confronted* with its being and function. When we have to figure it out in order to use it, in order for it to work, lest it stay broken and stuck. In the case of a door, we normally aren't confronted with a door's being and function because it works seamlessly. But when a door breaks, suddenly we are forced to contend with its door-ness, so we can eventually return it to a state where we no longer need to think about it anymore, and the door becomes ready-to-hand again. I.e., almost invisible, fulfilling its normal use, and functioning the way it's supposed to.

Speaking of doors, one time when my ex-husband's brother was visiting us, he got stuck outside our apartment. The lock for our front door suddenly wouldn't turn no matter how we jiggled the key. My brother-in-law needed to get inside and we needed to get out. We tried everything we could think of, but nothing worked. Hours passed as we mounted one effort after another to no avail, my brother-in-law in the hallway of my building by the elevator, us inside half laughing, half becoming very concerned we were going to have to take the door off the hinges. Occasionally it crossed my mind—what if there was a fire? What would we do? The apartment was on the sixth floor so there would be no going out the window.

Finally, we did what we should have done immediately: we called a locksmith. We delayed this obvious step because we knew it would be expensive. We lived in New York City, after all. The locksmith arrived, he said there was no fixing the lock, so he replaced it. The door was fixed, my brother-in-law got inside, we got out, and all was well, except for the fact that it did cost a lot, more even than we'd anticipated. But afterward we laughed about the whole ordeal. Then we all went back to forgetting about the door because it was working again, and so the door was ready-to-hand once more. The door was being itself. Hooray!

But it's one thing when a door breaks and becomes present-at-hand and we need to contend with it, and a whole other problem when it's *our being* that breaks and becomes present-at-hand and we need to contend with it. For Heidegger, our being is normally ready-to-hand for us, too, just like those doors and our cars (hopefully) and every other object we regularly pick up and use in our lives—a water glass, a pencil, the socks we put on in the morning, and the forks we use to eat our spaghetti for lunch. But just like everything else that might break or suddenly lose its regular function, our being can unfortunately do this, too. When our being is the thing that suddenly becomes present-at-hand, we are in trouble. This is how Heidegger understands and explains existential angst, that plummet into the abyss. It's the experience of our normal, everyday functioning suddenly no longer working, no longer making sense. When our being shifts from present-at-hand to ready-to-hand, we become paralyzed in a state of existential anxiety. Heidegger makes no bones about the seriousness of this, either: to arrive in such a place is a kind of torment, which can jeopardize a person's will to do anything. For Heidegger, it's also possible that once we plummet, once our being becomes ready-to-hand, we may never find our way out.

But while we can take our cars to a mechanic, we can buy new socks when they get holes, and we can call a locksmith to fix our doors, it's not so easy to resolve when it's our being that breaks down. Of course, now we'd probably go straight to therapy if we are fortunate enough to have the means and the insurance to help. But Heidegger was not writing during the time of regular access to therapy, and in college I still wasn't living during that time, either.

Remember how during my first semester at Georgetown I said it was as though Sartre had reached across space and time and all that darkness to give me the words to describe what I was going through? Well, this happens again during my Heidegger seminar and it happens big-time for me. When I learn about these two concepts, a lightbulb goes on in my brain that is never extinguished. That still hasn't gone out all these decades later. I am suddenly equipped with new concepts to apply to what I've been regularly experiencing over the course of college, because it sure does seem like it's my being that keeps becoming present-at-hand for me again and again.

This explains everything, I think to myself. This is what I've been suffering.

When I plunge into the abyss, my whole being becomes present-at-hand, like a doorknob that falls off and onto the floor when I'm trying to walk into a room. Something that has previously worked without effort is suddenly broken and forcing me to try and make sense of it. Yet without the right tools, I can't. My being will just stay broken. So the million-dollar question for me becomes: How does Heidegger think we solve for our being? How does a person get out of a state of existential anxiety after falling into it? Especially since it can leave a person fairly catatonic?

I wanted answers. I wanted fixes. I wanted hope.

If any prayer was going on in me during my senior year at Georgetown, my prayers were going out to Heidegger.

This is also where Heidegger gets very tricky, and I spend many months during college trying to come up with metaphors to show

how solving for one's being works for him. His answer in *Being and Time* is pretty frustrating. He basically says: There is no clear way through. But we simply and suddenly find our way out. Kind of like when I was on that bridge: one moment I couldn't move and was completely and totally paralyzed, the next I was walking again. For Heidegger, we just suddenly find ourselves functioning again. We find ourselves having moved through the anxiety and out the other side.

I know. What? Not so helpful or specific.

The wonder of this for Heidegger is that if we manage to find our way out again, we are changed because of it. Completely transformed. An ontological shift has occurred. Our experience of the world and our place within it has been altered permanently, as is our sense of being and meaning. Because we've experienced an acute bout of existential angst, we now know what it is to lose all sense of ourselves, so when it comes back to us, we also acutely feel it. We never quite go back to our being as present-at-hand again, not like it was before, but we are able to operate and move and function and put on our socks and go through doors and eat our spaghetti with forks and spoons or, gulp, even knives if you are not actually Italian.

I wrote an entire paper on this shift for Heidegger based on the haunting movie *The Piano*. I remember going to see it in the theater and both loving it and also being traumatized by it. Spoiler alert: the movie is a very dark love story about a very disturbed man played by Harvey Keitel, and a gifted pianist played by Holly Hunter. Long story short: in a fit of rage, Harvey Keitel cuts off Holly Hunter's finger and she is emotionally destroyed, given that her life's meaning is based on her music and her playing (think Sartre's Bad Faith). There is a scene at the end, where Keitel is rowing a rather catatonic Hunter in a boat along with her piano and she wants the piano thrown overboard. When it's pushed off the side of the boat, she tangles her foot into the rope around it and is flung down into the sea along with it, presumably because without the ability to play the piano herself, she has lost the will to live and would rather drown. We watch as she plummets down, down, the piano dragging her toward the bottom. Then suddenly, inexplicably, and out of nowhere, she awakens out of that catatonic state, and starts struggling to free her foot from the rope, eventually doing so and swimming mightily to the surface. She breaks through, gasping, alive.

I watched this film during the same semester as my Heidegger seminar. When I saw this scene, I thought: That's it! This is what Heidegger meant by how we just suddenly find ourselves coming out of existential anxiety, how we just find ourselves moving through the world again, and making sense of our being. We lose the will but then, rather miraculously, it floods us once more, and we gasp to life again above the surface of all that darkness.

My problem, of course, is that I keep going overboard, lifeless, unmoving, paralyzed, I fall down and down and down. Then suddenly and inexplicably, out of nowhere I am kicking like mad, lungs screaming, trying to get back to the surface again so I can breathe. I am caught in this cycle. But I always manage to get through it. The more I read philosophers like Heidegger, the less I feel alone in this, and the more words and concepts I acquire to apply to whatever it is I'm experiencing. Words and concepts I can use to answer to anyone who asks what is going on with me when I plummet. I want permanent fixes, but at least now I have something, a kind of explanation. And at least there seems to always be a way through, I just need to stay there and endure until my legs start to kick, seemingly of their own volition. But I still wish for a more scientific path, a tried-and-true means for prevention. What I want is a cure. A permanent cure. Something that will turn me into a different person, someone William James might give the label healthy-minded.

Over the years I will get used to the darkness within me, accept that its residence is permanent, that it will never leave me. I learn to live with it because I must. I have no choice.

15

Crossroads.

Before my graduation from Georgetown, as many of my peers are getting ready to go off and be doctors and lawyers and investment bankers, as they prepare for careers that will make them money nearly immediately after leaving college, I am busy getting even more serious about philosophy.

By now, I know I want a PhD. I feel it all the way to my bones. I want a PhD with my whole heart and soul, it's the kind of wanting I usually reserve for a boyfriend. Something I feel I need like my life depends on it. And this is the thing: I do feel like my life depends on getting my doctorate. Just like as a child, when I would sit on the floor while my father taught me algebra and solving for x as we played with Legos, as I near the end of my time at Georgetown, I am trying to solve for the x that is the darkness in my brain, my body, my soul. Philosophy is the only true balm I have found to soothe it.

I'm not ready to let it go. In fact, I never want to. I want to become a philosopher myself.

As it turns out, the darkness in me is very intellectually motivating. And the effort to rescue myself from a lifetime of being stuck in the abyss makes for good grades, and turns me into one of those students who goes above and beyond in her studies. A student always sitting in the visitor's chair in her professors' offices, one lucky enough to find many professors at Georgetown happy to have her there, talking about ideas and questions and theory. And of course I am motivated. I am there to search for my own salvation, a secret passageway out of the abyss, a trapdoor that will send me shooting upward toward the living again. I am sure a PhD will lead me to even more answers. A whole lifetime of reading and doing philosophy would be ideal for this. I am like someone with a mysterious yet chronic illness, on the hunt for a cure, who will stop at nothing until I find it, until I have the pills in my hand that will finally alleviate what is ailing me.

But something else becomes exciting to me, too: the idea of sharing my love for philosophy with others, with students like myself one day. The fantasy of what my future could look like begins to coalesce and become clear and I am thrilled. I want to become a professor of philosophy, like my own beloved professors who I see as instrumental to my salvation, and in helping me find my true joy, which involves reading across the whole history of the discipline. I want to one day become them. So I can someday teach philosophy to people like me.

Maybe you're laughing about what I want for myself here: to be an evangelist of sorts—but of Sartre and Heidegger and Nietzsche. Kierkegaard, too. To preach the Gospel of Camus. So like my mother and yet also so not. I can see this so clearly now, even if I couldn't back then.

By the time I finish Georgetown, I've also grown to see that there is so much life in me. I am still my mother's daughter after all, as much as I am my father's. I fluctuate between residing in the abyss and also residing on the cobblestone streets of Georgetown, having a good time, careening down the sidewalk with my roommates in shopping carts, cooking pasta with way too much garlic for friends in the middle of the night, dating boys and going to parties and even being a Georgetown cheerleader. But one thing I never stop doing is throwing my whole heart and soul into my studies. Philosophy has become that lifeline my mother wants for me so badly even though it isn't the specific lifeline she offered. I grab on to it and hold tight, and for a while it is enough.

But then, how does a person like me—a self-professed fundamentalist atheist during college—end up in graduate school getting her doctorate in religious studies and theology? Because that is what ends up happening when I go to get that PhD. My doctorate isn't in philosophy after all, though I will explore these programs in my search for the right graduate school. A search that takes me first to many alternative places, the possibility of getting my degree at the University of Santa Clara's History of Consciousness program, or even the Committee on Social Thought at U Chicago—a place I almost go when I get in. But something keeps stopping me and I don't end up there. Those places aren't quite right for me, and I know this to my gut.

Then one day I am in a favorite professor's office. It is long and narrow, and she has a warm lamp lit instead of the cold, fluorescent lights overhead. As usual, I am in her visitor's chair. I am often in her visitor's chair even after I graduate and am no longer a student. She is one of my favorite people. Tiny, energetic, so alive, her brain bubbling with the joy of ideas, warm, friendly, her hair cropped short, glasses always on, her lips always with a smile, her demeanor always welcoming. We are talking about where I should apply for graduate school, what I should apply for, and she poses a question—carefully, gently, because she knows me well.

"Did you realize all of your philosophical questions are religious in nature?"

Her words cause me to go still. The lamplight glows around and behind her, I can see the trees beyond her office window, the bookshelves lining the wall top to bottom, as familiar as my own room I am there so often. But suddenly I am disoriented. I cannot move. I am uncharacteristically silent. But my brain is churning.

I've never considered this possibility, not since I became a fundamentalist atheist. Why would I give any thought to religion, when religion is the thing that failed me, when God had only shown God's absence, when I've experienced only abandonment as I wallow in the darkness? It's true, the questions I asked in my philosophy major were always the Biggest Questions of all, the kind that require the use of capital letters, questions not just of meaning but of Meaning, not just of relationship but of Relationship. Yet I've always arrived at the Nothing, not the Something. God has never been in the picture of my future. I cannot see why God would have anything to do with my doctorate. And yet now that she mentions this, I also can kind of see her point.

So "No," I tell her at first. Then add, "Well, maybe."

During this moment in my professor's office, I admit to myself that I haven't truly thought my questions through to their obvious ends, or I've always stopped them short from getting there. Maybe I've been doing this on purpose. Maybe I've been avoiding going there all this time. But now that my professor put this out there, and laid it down in full view between us—my trusted, beloved professor who knows my brain and my intellect and my ideas and all the things that move me as well as I know them myself, someone I worship, someone I adore—as I sit in the visitor's chair next to her desk like always, I realize she is right.

She leans toward me, elbows on the armrest. "My father writes about religion, you know."

I do not know—not until now.

"He's written many books about his questions, which are much like yours, Donna. He's a professor, too." She turns around and pulls a book off the shelf and hands it to me—one of her father's.

I look at it, wanting to open it immediately, appreciating this act of intimacy on my professor's part, a sharing of something so dear to her with me, a handing over of her father's words and ideas in order to help me sort out my own. A seeing something of her father in me, her former student. An honor bestowed upon my person. I hold it carefully, reverently, realizing the gift that it is. "I didn't know your father was also a professor like you," I say out loud.

"Why don't you read this and see what you think," she tells me. "Your ideas are broader than the academic discipline of philosophy. They're interdisciplinary. In religious studies you can go all over. You can study literature, psychology, you can pull from all the humanities. The people around you will also be asking many of the same questions you are. And I worry that a traditional philosophy program would stifle you."

I am still looking at her father's book, feeling the weight of it in my hands, eager to read it the second I leave her office, curious what I will find when I do. What her father is like, if I will see her in him somehow, in his words, what they'll say. "Okay," I agree, because I have no qualms about putting my life and future in her hands.

"And Donna," she says before I leave, "I think you'd be happier studying religion, too."

I read her father's book, I read it and love it. I start to investigate religious studies programs, theology programs, divinity school and divinity degrees. While so much of it feels unfamiliar and not like me—I don't want to be a pastor, I've never thought about becoming a theologian or a professor of theology, I'm a woman so it's not like I can become a Catholic priest, and besides, I am an atheist—I can see why she suggested the possibility. I find myself excited about the classes offered in the coursebooks, about the specializations of the professors, about their interests and areas of study. I can see their roots in philosophy, too, how philosophy and theory underpin it all. But also literature and sociology and social justice and psychology, and most importantly, I can see how these professors and their work are so very rooted in the world, the everyday, the practical tools we need to survive living, to live a good life, to make sense of our own humanity. The stuff I love the most from my philosophy major but also the stuff that most of the other philosophy majors didn't find interesting themselves. While they often stopped with theory, I always kept going with the how and the why in the practical application of it all. I was always the philosophy student taking the ideas and theories and trying to drag them down to earth, to the stuff that is the work of living, to make sense of the ideas in the everyday actions of our world.

This is exactly what my professor's father is doing in all of his work. I fly through his books, get copies of my own. I still have them. I start reading the books of other religion professors and theologians from these programs and soon begin to believe that there is a place for me in this field. I grow even more excited, more certain. I've found my future and I can't wait for it to start.

I call my parents. "I'm going to apply for a PhD in Religious Studies."

"What?"

"Yes. It's what I want."

To say that my mother and father are surprised by this turn in my interests, with this news I offer, is the understatement of a lifetime. After all, I am their outspoken, fundamentalist atheist daughter by this point. *"Really?"*

"Definitely," I tell first my father and then my mother as they pass the phone between them. "You can be an atheist, you know, and study religion," I go on.

They're not buying it, however. "Okaayyyy?"

"Really."

"Whatever you think, sweetheart," my mother says eventually.

But my parents are perplexed. They will stay that way for years about this shift in my path. Maybe even for the rest of their lives. I'm not sure they ever make sense of it.

I apply to many programs, I get into most of them, and I get funding to pay for my degree, too. I agonize over where to go because I love living in Georgetown and I don't want to leave. It feels like my home now, my happy place, where I have a wonderful social network and great friends and where I love walking the streets and going to the restaurants and being so close to where I became an intellectual person in the first place. I am a little afraid, too, of going somewhere completely new where I have none of these things, no stability, no network, no familiar places that I love and feel like home, no close friends to speak of. I fear the earthquake this could become for me.

So I turn down Ivy League offers of placement and funding, and instead find myself leaning toward attending the most Catholic school I've applied to, despite how somewhere in the corner of my brain this fact gives me pause. But I push this unease aside and focus on how the Catholic University of America is just across the city from Georgetown. I can drive there in twenty minutes, I won't even have to move apartments. My life can stay exactly as it is in Georgetown, with all the things I love about it, except that it will have an added thing I adore, which is graduate school, studying for my doctorate. Hooray!

Besides, the dean at Catholic U really, really wants me there. He shares my questions and my weirdness, he even knows about my atheism and still wants me to be a part of his program. I am different than his typical student, he tells me, and he wants this for the people who will be my peers. I think he wants me there, too, because he and I are a lot alike in our thinking, and as I'll soon find out, we have similar struggles. He will become one of the greatest mentors I'll ever have in my lifetime, and also the person who will help to save me from the one terrible, also life-changing thing that will befall me while I am a student in his program.

And this man, the professor who will become my newest mentor, needs my answer.

Do I want to attend his program or not?

My response becomes a fatal crossroad of sorts, though I don't know this yet.

"Yes," I tell him excitedly over the phone one day.

Absolutely yes.

If my childhood was marked by that earthshaking realization that there were other gods, followed by me saying *Yup, nope, faith is just not for me*—then graduate school becomes the time when things get serious, when my lack of belief in God begins to feel like life or death. When I set out on a mission to find God, come hell or high water. The mission of a lifetime. My lifetime.

And if college was the time I became a fundamentalist atheist, my twenties are the time I become something else, though I'm not sure what to call myself exactly. Someone who finally stops telling her mother that God is Santa Claus, for sure, yet not someone who calls herself a believer, either. But definitely someone who begins to respect the faith and beliefs of the very faithful people I soon find around me in my classes. Though not someone who can identify herself among that flock, either. But I begin to hope for a different outcome next time I fall down into the abyss—to find a *something* instead of *nothing* amid all my darkness. I am so serious about trying to find *something*, I go so far as to get a PhD in this effort.

And even if I didn't want to admit this out loud back then, not even to my mother, I knew that each time I stared down into that black hole of despair, there remained a tiny hope that this time I would feel the cushion of God's arms carrying me out of the darkness like some sort of fireman's rescue. My existential anxiety taught me from experience that no one was coming to rescue me, no one named God or Jesus, at least—at least, not so far—but I wanted to be proven wrong. I would never stop searching to be proven wrong, either. Getting my doctorate was evidence of this, a cloak that once I'd shrugged it over my shoulders I would never remove. I am still wearing it now, all these years later.

Very soon during the best of times, when things are good in my life and I am being both my mother's daughter and my father's, too, I begin putting my whole self toward the end of understanding religious experience, exactly what the experience of God is and looks like and feels like—from the people who guide their lives with such an incredible spiritual rudder. People like my own mother, for example. Very soon my reading habits will collide with William James and those sick souls of his research, among other healthier religious folks, and I will read and reread as I try, desperately, to understand. And even amid all the terrible things that will soon befall me at the hands of one of my future professors while I am getting my PhD, I will still find the energy to chase down reports that God is alive and well, at least for some people. I will read mystic after mystic, all the spiritual figures I can find, anyone and everyone who can speak of knowing God, of having experienced God's reality, of believing that God is real.

I want God to be real.

Even if it takes me a while to admit it, I come to envy all of these believers. I want to be them.

Deep down even in my most fervent atheist days, I think I still always knew I didn't want to be an atheist in the long run, that an atheist's life was not the life for me, and I would do anything to change this part of me. Anything at all.

Part IV
So Many Elephants

16

I find out Teresa of Ávila and Jesus are total feminists.

I arrive at grad school wide-eyed and excited.

There is a reception for new students, replete with wine, industrial cheese cubes, my future professors and peers. I choose my favorite sundress for the occasion. It's August in DC after all, still hot out, the blacktop steaming. On my way across the city to campus, I maneuver my car through all the stoplights, the unfamiliar streets and turns that I will soon know so well I can make them by sheer instinct. I park in the lot, I get out, I straighten my long dress and head inside the big stone building that houses my future department, my new academic home, the place I'll spend the next five years studying and thinking and asking questions as I pursue my doctorate. Where I'll begin the latest version of my search for Meaning.

My heart races as I enter the room for the event, I can feel it pounding in my chest. I am not the youngest person here but I'm close, and I'm definitely the only one dressed fashionably, in a way I'd characterize as especially feminine. When I look around me, I see mainly attire that is reserved, understated, and more than this, religious. There are priests and nuns in various kinds of robes and habits and collars. I am the odd woman out for sure.

But soon I am meeting professors and I relax. Armed with a glass of red wine, I make my way around the room, introducing myself. I am never more my mother's daughter than at a party.

One professor, older, quick with a wry smile, eyes as alive as those of my mother, begins a conversation with me—first with small talk, but soon our conversation about hometowns and other basic, personal details gives way to a lively discussion about Heidegger. Heidegger already! We discuss whether he was a philosopher and also a poet. Within minutes I feel at home, I *am* at home, and a single conversation with this professor becomes a door opening, an invitation for me to be me, confirmation I've arrived at the place I'm meant to be. When I find out this professor will be teaching one of my classes that semester, my heart soars. I am open, I am alive, I am ready to begin, I am full of hope, I am in my happy place. I may be dressed differently than everyone else, but I am still among my people—people who live to read, who love to think, as much as I do. People searching just like I am. People like this funny, wry, smiling professor.

Sure, many of these people, maybe even most, are also priests, monks, nuns, priests-in-training, nuns-in-training, novitiates, friars, people who've taken different kinds of vows. Or people who were once going to be priests but then decided against it, or people still contemplating becoming a priest, like the fellow student who'll become one of my lifelong, closest friends. Or the peers much older than I am, men and women who've lived entire lives, had families, other professions and careers, and who decided to pursue study later on, after they figured out what truly means something to them. Or people who used to be nuns, like so many of my mother's friends from the beach.

This is the thing about the world where I land, and where I find myself getting my PhD: Even though I am very different from my fellow students, I am also quickly at home among them. They aren't that different from the people who populated the actual home of my childhood, my life growing up with someone like my mother; where it was just as common to sit in a bathing suit building a sandcastle with a nun nearby, or an ex-nun, or to even run into the parish priest going for a walk down by the water. Just as it was totally normal to see nuns and priests at my school or my mother's school or to have dinner with them at our kitchen table. In grad school, I've come full circle, because once again I'm surrounded by people openly Catholic, openly devout, openly searching and doubting and dabbling and professing on the subject of faith.

I am very open about my atheism, too. It makes some people blink when they hear me discuss this part of my identity, or wince a little, but mainly people accept where I am. They accept who I am. They ask lots of questions, but no one rejects me. They hang in as I struggle and doubt and question openly. It's also true that if there is a spectrum of believers in my program and at one end is Atheist, the other Devout Believer, I am all alone way over there, standing under the Atheist moniker. So in a way, I am isolated. But I am still here.

The door feels open wide to me and the truth of all that I am. I don't feel I need to hide anything so I don't—the opposite, in fact. Head held high, smiling, I walk straight on in as myself to this new chapter of my life, eager, enthusiastic, thrilled really, and I don't look back.

"I'm not a feminist."

This is a phrase I used to love to lob at my gender studies–minoring roommate at Georgetown. I often followed it up with a rather sinister *muahaha* of laughter. I loved to poke at her about the topic and my rejection of the label. It drove her crazy. My college roommate was getting a minor only because that's all Georgetown offered when we were students. If there had been a gender studies major, she would have become one.

But me? I was philosophy all the way, as you know. And when I wasn't stuck in the abyss, I was doing other things—super-girly things. Like getting yearly subscriptions to *Vogue* and *Elle* and every other women's fashion magazine in existence. Wearing heels with everything I owned, paired with short skirts and all kinds of other fashionable outfits. (At least at the time, I fancied myself very high fashion.) I loved shopping, I loved to search for designer bargains at T.J. Maxx, I loved wearing lipstick and mascara and all kinds of jewelry. I disassociated all of these qualities in myself with being a feminist.

In other words, during my undergraduate years I did that totally clichéd thing young women used to do—maybe still do? Which is to assume if I was girly and liked pink (I do!) and wore high heels and loved boys (that, too!), then I couldn't be a feminist. Somehow my very intellectual philosophy brain was unable to hold in tension this notion that I could be both a feminist and wear high heels. All this to say, I was really young and naïve about the whole feminist enterprise.

So there I am in graduate school, somehow landing myself at one of the most Catholic universities in the country, and I arrive with absolutely zero interest in feminism. It's not even a concept I think about. Never mind feminism in a theological context. I am just disinterested in the topic. As far as I'm concerned, gender and feminism have nothing to do with my dogged pursuit of the divine and its nature, of religious experience and what it looks like and how it shows up in the everyday lives of humans and whether it is all real or a bunch of bull.

Then I end up with these women professors who are, like, "Jesus was a feminist, by the way."

And at first, I am, like, "Who cares?"

At first. Because eventually I start to care. Soon I care *a lot*.

My first year at graduate school, I signed up for pretty much all the courses taught by the women in my program because, why not? Those courses lined up alongside other courses about medieval mystics, which had syllabi that included a good dose of women thinkers and writers, because a lot of the most famous medieval mystics are women like Julian of Norwich and Teresa of Ávila. But as with feminist Jesus, I was skeptical of the women mystics, too. They spoke way too much about their embrace of suffering as a path to God (don't girls and women already suffer enough?), and then they'd given up sex for a life of seclusion and celibacy. This was definitely not a path that held any interest for me, since I was not about to take up a life of no sex. So what really did these medieval women have to offer someone who didn't want to become a nun? Not much, as far as I was concerned.

But then I began to hear another story about how to understand these women, one that made me listen hard: the version where these women showed themselves to be quite rebellious on the religion front. Rebellious in a way I admired. I started to see them not as lady tools of the Church, but as spiritual rebels, women thwarting the status quo of an historical era which told them they were nothing more than baby-making chattel, the property of men, not even worthy of an education. Now I began to see them as the extraordinary women they were: women who defied the norms of their time, who became nuns and gained access to an education and literacy because of this, who skirted the endless, dangerous childbearing years that killed so many of their contemporaries by becoming celibate, avoiding marriage to a man who might put them in this dangerous position and treat them like property to boot. Through their pursuit of God, these women claimed a direct line to the divine and in doing so gained a shocking amount of power within a church, culture, and time where women were meant to have none. These women went and got themselves power, and then they weren't afraid to use it. And many of them (like Hildegard of Bingen, to name one) used it to tell the men of their day what to do and believe and what was up! And they did this in the name of God!

Maybe I'd judged them too quickly?

Meanwhile, I was also reading books in my other courses with titles like *She Who Is* about the feminine divine, reading women scholars positing feminine language and metaphors for the trinity, many of them Catholic nuns. Catholic scholar-nuns. Even though at first I wasn't interested in considering Jesus much at all, never mind in a feminist context, I bent my ear when my professors proposed that we should imagine a woman's body on the cross to see where it landed us spiritually. And though I'd always been more interested in the most abstract ideas about God and the divine, suddenly this physical, oh so feminine talk of God and Jesus got my attention and held it.

For years my mother tried to talk to me about the idea of God as a woman. Of course I rolled my eyes at her. She doggedly continued to raise the possibility and I doggedly continued to shrug in response. It took someone completely outside my family to convince me that maybe what my mother suggested held some merit. If my mother had been the one to hand me Julian of Norwich or Hildegard of Bingen or Teresa of Ávila, the nun with the sword, fighting her way to God against the devils residing inside her, I probably would have handed these ladies right back to her. But it wasn't my mother, it was someone else, so I was willing to open these books and take a

look at what these women had to say. And what they said turned out
to change my life and all that I believe about the world, and maybe
even God within it.

Listen, I have never been a good rule follower.

Not as a kid, much to my mother's dismay, and definitely not as
a teenager, as proven by all those times when my parents told me
to stay home and I went out the window at night. And definitely not
during college, as proven by my philosophy major (again to my poor
parents' dismay) and the ridiculous stuff I did all the time, like refusing to wear shoes for a solid month during my first year of Georgetown (let's not focus too long on that one).

All this to say: I tended to go outside the lines in all kinds of
ways, sometimes silly, sometimes serious. And to me, Catholicism
had always been about rule following. Constricting a person, rob-
bing her of choice, and even of her curious brain. Though I'd loved
the Jesuits at Georgetown and all the room they made for my doubts,
I still understood the Catholic tradition as a faith of obedience. A
faith of nonthinking sheep. I considered myself an intellectual
thinker, someone who defied norms, so I couldn't imagine myself
among its flock. It was a tradition without a place for someone like
me. Or that's what I told myself.

Then I met these Catholic ladies. Some were still alive, some were
long dead, some of them were my professors, many of them were
nuns, and all of them were rule breakers. Think Nadia Bolz-Weber,
Rachel Held Evans, Sarah Bessey, but the Catholic version of these
women, albeit a lot older and possibly celibate. Women who, when
Catholicism didn't seem to have or want to make space for them, or
allow them an honest, true voice to speak what they believed, or give
them any power or position at all, they were, like, *Nope, not going
away!* Then they went and cleared a space for themselves and took

up residence there and said what they had to say, and boy, was it powerful.

I followed up Julian of Norwich and Teresa of Ávila with Dorothy Day and Dorothee Soelle and then Simone Weil. The fervent beliefs and religious language of these women alienated me sometimes, but I also couldn't get them out of my system. Most importantly, many of them talked about an experience that named something so familiar to me, something we apparently all shared and that I'd always believed was exclusively the stuff of existentialist philosophers. These were the women who first introduced me to the Dark Night of the Soul.

St. John of the Cross may be the most famous person to write on the topic of the Dark Night, but it was his contemporary St. Teresa of Ávila who reached inside me and took up residence within my heart on this subject. I began to wonder if her Dark Night was akin to the abyss that kept pulling me down into that sea of existential despair. It sure sounded like it. But for Teresa, the journey into the Dark Night and out of it again was spiritual and heroic in nature. An experience of being very far from God, being lost to God, where a person suffers a total absence of God, even a wholesale abandonment by God. A time when a person loses sight of God to the point where they question everything, where faith seems impossible. As I read Teresa, I thought, *Yes. Yes I know what you're talking about.* Her Dark Night seemed to get its darkness from what I'd learned to call existential despair—a chilling loneliness, a kind of vertigo of one's being. But for these mystics and spiritual thinkers, already people of faith, the plummet was sparked by a losing sight of the God of that faith.

I felt recognized, I found new words, I was less alone.

So I kept reading these women, diving deep into their journeys of the soul, not quite sure where they'd lead me, or if I might find God at the end of this road. I felt them hanging on to me, and this I cherished. It was as if Teresa of Ávila marched across the room when she saw me looking through the window of her convent and threw open the door, ushering me inside. Then she cleared a space for me to sit at her table, pointed, and said:

"This is a place just for you, Donna Freitas."

When I hesitated to sit, in unfamiliar territory as I was, she nodded in understanding. "Don't worry, I'm saving this spot. It will still be here when you are ready."

Once again, a hand was reaching out to me through the darkness of my existential angst, but this time it wasn't the hand of Sartre or Camus or even Heidegger. It was the sword-wielding hand of Teresa of Ávila as she fought her way to God through the dark and into the light, pulling me along behind her. On another occasion it became the wounded hand of Julian of Norwich, reaching through the narrow window of the abbey cell where she lived and prayed. Suddenly I could hear the voices of so many other contemporary nuns, too, who were writing about the feminine body of God, the feminine divine, the feminist Jesus and her wounded body. A whole table full of fierce, outspoken women, many of them still alive and claiming the title feminist for themselves. Beckoning me to join them at their table, too, which turned out to be the same one as Teresa's. Offering me a chair. Pulling it out for me.

I found myself wanting to say yes and take a seat.

I began to listen, ever more closely. Even though I'd been invited to this table of faith and church so many times before, I'd never been invited in a way that made me wish to stay. Yet now I heard a new story that described this experience that had so long afflicted me, yet such a different version than Sartre had offered.

The Dark Night of the Soul had a vastly different ending than the one I'd gotten from the philosophers of my undergraduate years, and this difference was crucial. Whereas for Sartre and his peers, on the other side of the abyss there was only nothingness, for these spiritual thinkers, on the other side of the soul's Dark Night was God. A kind of spiritual rebirth. Life, our relationships, our work were not merely screens hiding us from the abyss and the nothing, instead these things were imbued with a divine significance and beauty. When our very beings became present-at-hand to us, as Heidegger might put it, and when we could no longer make sense of our place in the world, for these women and spiritual thinkers, their nights grew dark because they lost sight of something real and true and meaningful—and not the other way around.

This was the first time I became suspicious of Sartre's notion of Bad Faith. When I realized there might be other ways of looking at my own darkness, when I began to question whether I'd had the wrong lens for seeing the world and myself this whole time; when it occurred to me that looking through the lens of these women instead of Sartre and Nietzsche might help me understand the darkness inside me much differently. That maybe on the other side of all that nothingness was actually *something*. Something real and important and life-giving. Something like love and hope and justice and newness. Human flourishing. Connection. Not nothing at all.

Maybe even, the call of God. The call of God *to me*.

I must admit: a good part of me was still very skeptical.

But I was also *in*.

I wanted to understand better what these women meant.

So apparently the term *feminist* did apply to me.

I should have told my mother.

She would have been thrilled.

17

The only way through is to skip ahead.

My mother used to fantasize about being a Walmart greeter.

We didn't have a Walmart in Rhode Island for ages because everybody in our tiny state fought the building of one for about a million different reasons. But Walmart eventually won this battle, and so the Walmart eventually opened. And like everyone else who's ever lived in a fairly sleepy place where anything new is a thrill, my parents got in the car and drove down to see what the fuss was all about. Then my mother called to make her report to me after the fact.

"Sweetheart, your father and I went to see the Walmart," she said.

I laughed. "And how was it, Mom? Was it all you hoped for?"

"Big. It was very big. But I found my new job."

"You have a job, Mom. You're a nursery school teacher."

"Yes, but this is going to be what I do now."

"And what is this job?"

"A Walmart greeter."

Walmart greeters?

"What are you talking about, Mom?"

At the time of this phone call, I had very little experience with Walmarts or too many other big-box stores, so I truly had no idea what my mother meant.

"Donna," she went on, "at Walmart, there are these people who just stand at the door, welcoming you. They smile, they say hello, they ask if you need help, they hand you a basket."

"Okaaaay," I said. Meanwhile I was trying to figure out how serious my mother was about this new dream job of hers. In truth, a part of me was thinking my mother would make a fantastic Walmart greeter, given the way she described the position. She had all the right qualifications: She smiled a lot, she was super friendly, and sincerely so. She was nothing if not helpful, and her energy for laughter and chatting randomly with anybody who came near her was endless. Walmart would be lucky to have a greeter like my mother.

"What's this really about, Mom?"

There came a pause on the other end of the line. Then, "I just like the idea that there is a job where you stand at the door and greet people nicely when they're coming inside."

I could tell she was still holding back. "Aaaannnd? What else?"

She sighed. "I'm getting kind of tired, sweetheart. Teaching is so exhausting. I don't know how long I can keep up with doing it."

"But you love teaching."

"Of course I do. But I think being a Walmart greeter would be fun!"

"Okay, Mom," I demurred.

As it would turn out, my mother's exhaustion was due to the still-undiagnosed fourth-stage ovarian cancer metastasizing through her body. It's also true that teaching is an exhausting, exacting profession regardless of whether you are sick and dying while doing it. But even after my mother's diagnosis and even though she would literally end up teaching nursery school until the day she died, she never stopped talking about being a greeter. The only thing that changed was that her possible place of employment expanded to include Target. Apparently Target also employed happy greeters, something I learned after one of those opened in Rhode Island, too. My mother informed me of this after her initial visit when, just as before with the Walmart, my parents got in the car and made their way over to see what the fuss was all about with Target. For my mother, her biggest takeaway was that Target was another store which employed greeters.

"Maybe when I retire, this is what I'm going to do," she told me on a different call. "I think I'd enjoy it. I think I'd be *good* at it."

I pictured my mother, the light in her eyes that was always there, the joy on her face that made the little nursery school children adore her and do whatever she told them to, the way my mother was so good at welcoming people somewhere, anywhere, be it to her classroom or our house or at church on Sundays. I told her then, "I'm sure you would be great, Mom."

My mother never fulfilled her dream of being a greeter of a Walmart or a Target or any other store employing greeters. Every time I walk into one of these stores today and someone greets me at the door with a hello and a smile, I think of her, I imagine her standing there, chatting everybody up. Exclaiming excitedly about every small child who passes by and helping the elderly with a patience few other people I've known can boast.

Here is the thing about my mom: She *was* kind of a greeter during her lifetime—for the Catholic Church. She was like a one-woman Catholic welcome wagon.

She was really good at this, too. She loved her church, she loved her faith, she loved the priests and the nuns and the pomp and the circumstance and the communion of saints and all the rituals and the incense and every moment of the liturgical calendar. She loved receiving the Eucharist on Sundays and being a Eucharistic minister herself and the sacraments and all things Catholic. My mother believed with her whole heart and soul that the Catholic Church was a force for good in the world. Her enthusiasm could not be dulled or dented or denied. She wore her love for this tradition on her sleeve, and her love for God and Jesus like every stitch of clothing in her wardrobe, including her sweaters that had flowers or ducks or dinosaurs knitted into them. The faith that was so vibrant in her burned so brightly, it sparked and crackled and lit her up as she moved through the world and announced her Catholic-ness to everybody.

My mother did her best to pass on this wholehearted love and joy about her faith to everyone around her, in her words and deeds and the way she lived her life. Like, the hills were alive with Jesus and God and the Holy Spirit for her, and if she'd been gifted an angelic voice like Julie Andrews, she would have sung it to all who'd listen and ushered them in by way of St. Peter's in Rome.

The Catholic Church was lucky to have such an excellent, enthusiastic greeter. Because another crucial thing you need to understand about Catholics, if you are Protestant and evangelical and reading this, it's that Catholics do not proselytize. We are the opposite of evangelical in this regard. We do not invite people to church on Sundays. Like, *we do not*—unless people specifically ask us for directions to the church because they're new in town and they're lost, and they've explained to us ahead of time they are a Catholic family looking for the parish hall and really, really need our help or will wander the town lost forever and church-less. We are very polite and restrained when it comes to speaking about our faith affiliations, because we would never want to impose. We are usually pretty closemouthed about it all. And we do not do any of this bring-people-to-Jesus stuff—that is the business of evangelical folk.

So just as we are not Bible readers, we are also not prone to evangelizing. Most of us are not good Walmart greeters for our tradition. Which made the way my mother was so open and enthusiastic and inviting when it came to church and her faith and her welcoming of everybody to it pretty unique. Especially welcoming to the people she loved the most, like me.

This brings me to the final thing I want to say about the Walmart greeter business and my mother doing such a good job for the Catholic Church over the course of her entire life out of the goodness of her heart and for no pay whatsoever:

It makes me want to scream and throw plates at the walls and break things.

Knowing all that I know now, I think this Catholic tradition my mother loved so much took advantage of people like her. They had the audacity to use people like her toward the end of maintaining a system and hierarchy that was rotten to its core and has behaved criminally on the level of the Mafia, an organization that covered up crimes against who knows how many thousands of people, how many thousands of *children*, one that even had a standard operating procedure for doing this very dirty business. Of course, the Catholic Church is not alone in behaving this way, since so many church traditions and communities and organizations have behaved this way, as we all now know—pastors and elders engaging in abuse and subsequent cover-ups, and coaches and teachers and schools and all kinds of other places and people doing the same. But the Catholic tradition is perhaps unique among them all in the breadth and scale of how they've sinned against their own people and against children, in particular.

It is rare for me to be thankful about my mother not living to see a certain moment in recent history, especially one that yours truly is involved with, because I miss her all the time. But I will be eternally grateful she did not live to see the abhorrent behavior of this church she loved so much over the course of these last twenty years, all the related crimes against children and other believers that have come to light and that went on during the decades while she was still alive. I am especially relieved she did not live to see the things this church perpetrated and continues to perpetrate against her own daughter, or at least, not the full effect of them. If the cancer hadn't killed her first, these things would surely have destroyed her instead. As they have so many others.

So, this is the unfortunate point in my story where the Catholic Church smashes into me, broadsiding my body in a way that will have me sinking for decades, trying to bail out the water that keeps threatening to drag me down to the bottom of the ocean. I will spend ages trying to pick out all the splinters littered across my skin. But this broadsiding doesn't happen only once, it happens and then keeps on happening and in many ways is still happening today, as I write these words. I am still trying to pick out all these splinters. New ones keep appearing.

If there is a mystery to my faith and my relationship to it—or lack thereof—this part of the story isn't that mysterious at all. It's not shocking or even surprising that what little whisper of faith survived underneath the veneer of my atheism, that tiny shoot of hope trying to break through the surface of my darkness during graduate school, would soon become walled off. Suffocated because of what I went through during grad school and while my mother was dying, despite all those nuns and lady scholars grabbing on to me and holding tight as everything around me was falling apart. A parallel experience kept pulling me from the grip of these women and pulling as hard as it could. I was no match for it nor were they.

Perhaps the greatest mystery of all is that the whisper left of my faith, my longing for it, my wish for God did somehow survive in spite of this violation of my person; it persisted and lingered even though I tried to kill it out of rage and despair about what happened to me, and I began to hate the possibility of faith and all that it touched because the wish for it also brought me such destruction.

What happened in grad school at the hands of one of Catholicism's many abusive priests is also why it is here I'm going to skip ahead to contemplate what happens in hindsight, rather than share it in the moment. There is no other way for me to process this particular juncture in my relationship to Catholicism and God but by looking backward at it, by doing my best to separate the terrible and the corrupt from the beautiful and the good that was the tradition my mother loved and wanted me to have with all the enthusiasm of a benevolent Walmart greeter.

I'm sure wherever my mother is, she would understand.

Maybe hand me a basket to help along the way.

18

Let's get the biggest elephant out of the way.

A couple of times, I've mentioned this "thing" that happened to me in graduate school. Well, here it is: I was stalked by a professor for years. He was also a Catholic priest. If you want to know all the gory details, I wrote an entire memoir devoted to it so you can get the full scoop there. But the most important things to know for this journey toward—and away from—faith for me, is the following:

My professor used my love of learning and my love of teachers as a way to get to me.

He also used my love for both my mother and my father.

*He used his vestments and his vows and the priesthood
as his cover.*

*He used the cancer and imminent death of my mother in
his efforts to insert himself into my life.*

*His behavior went on for so long and got so bad that I no
longer cared if I lived or died.*

His behavior started my very first semester because he taught one of my classes. He seemed to see something special in me, which made me feel chosen. But things devolved from there, and his invitations to continue the conversation we started during that initial class after our semester ended soon became inappropriate to the extreme.

His overtures included mountains of letters, unannounced visits to my apartment because he had access to my address in my student file, pleas that I go on a retreat with him to a secluded cabin, just the two of us, and soon near-constant phone calls and demands I meet him places. The worst of it involved the relationship he struck up with my mother because he also had access to my family's Rhode Island address and phone number in my student file.

Stupid me, I said nothing for a very long time, I just tried to endure his attention, partly because of the Catholic priest's vow of celibacy (this was before the abuse scandal broke). Also because he was the head of my concentration and one entire department. I didn't know how to get around him and still graduate with my PhD. It was like living under siege. Managing him was a 24-7 job and it got to a point where it was all I did. Finally, I confessed to a dear friend, also in my program, and he helped me get ready to come forward to ask for help, which was terrifying. Would I be believed?

Then came the other side of this nightmare, which swung around and hit me while I was already at rock bottom. The Catholic Church part, and their cover-up tactics.

By the time I told, I was so desperate for help with stopping this man from behaving this way toward me, I no longer cared if I lost my career or my life and my mother was already dying anyway. Again, stupid me, I believed people at my university would help to try and fix things. I was at a Catholic school, among very devout Catholics, so I assumed they'd want to help someone as broken and desperate and young as I was at the time. Also, I was obviously not at all okay, like on the surface of my body and face and in the expression of my eyes. I was melting down, shivering, worried I was going crazy. And I did find care and solace among certain professors. But the people in charge at my university—the higher-ups who were also higher-ups in the Catholic Church because of the university's vaulted role in relation to it—were only interested in the following:

Protecting the priest-professor.

Making the statute of limitations run out so I couldn't sue them.

Making sure I told no one else what happened.

Making me sign an NDA to enforce this legally on their and his behalf.

Keeping him teaching there.

Not long after all this, promoting him.

So on the higher levels of that university and its Catholic officials, I experienced zero kindness, care, or concern about my person, my education, my family, my dying mother, including about the way this professor used her cancer as yet another way to get to me. Nobody in the school's administration worried if I lived or died. Nobody worried whether I'd graduate or not. Nobody cared that I was destroyed and betrayed and traumatized and mortified and that I didn't know if I could go on or not. Nobody cared, either, that I would lose so much of myself to what this man did, including the future career I wanted, which was to be a professor.

At the time, I thought I must be the only person on this earth experiencing such a thing at the hands of a Catholic priest. When the abuse scandal eventually broke and unfolded and unfolded again and still unfolds today, I realized how not-alone I was that whole time. The scope of the abuse and cover-up is mind-numbing to me, as I'm sure it is to so many people. But in the coverage in the newspaper over the years, as I scoured the different articles, I began to recognize myself in what was done to others, because it was also done to me. Like running out the statute of limitations when a victim comes forward and doesn't realize a clock has started on her ability to pursue legal recourse. Like getting her to sign an NDA, then tossing her into the trash like she is garbage. This experience calls up many words into my throat and sometimes out of my mouth about these people and this tradition and how un-Jesus-like those who proclaim to stand in for Jesus can be.

To be clear:

The priest who did this to me wasn't the professor who recruited me to his graduate program and who became one of my most important mentors. It wasn't the professor who first talked to me at the welcome reception, either, the one with whom I discussed Heidegger as a poet. They, too, were both priest-professors like him. But they were wonderful, ready to help and be there for me. This was important for my relationship to priests in the long run. Even though a priest and a whole bunch of higher-ups who were also priests colluded to cover up what happened and cover me up in the process, there were other priests who extended their hand and fought for me against their peers in the effort to help me get through this and make it stop.

This allowed my respect for priests to survive.

And because I don't want this story of faith to become about them again—the people in the Catholic Church who betrayed me then and continue to betray me now—I'll cap this part of my story here. I am finished giving them that much power over my relationship to faith and God. They've had that power for far too long and it's time I yank it back. I want it to be mine again. I want to wash them clean of it. I want to wash my faith and my wish for God clean of *them*. I think I deserve that much after all this time.

Somehow my desire for faith survived all of this. It exists apart from and despite what happened. My wish for God, my longing for faith, my hope. And that seems pretty, seriously mysterious to me—like maybe the greatest mystery of all. Rather wondrous, really.

There's one other part of this story that's important to mention before moving forward.

When I first arrived at graduate school, as I began my deep dive into the philosophy of mystical and religious experience, the nature of spirituality, and began reading all those women thinkers, I was on the cusp of *something*—maybe something like a conversion. Nascent, sure, not very well formed, yes, and maybe I was still pretty uneasy and skeptical about it. But it is still there. It is literally right there on the pages I've written. When I see this evidence that *something* was happening inside me, unfurling, poking up, green and tender, and then I also know what comes next because of what this man did to me, and what the Church did on top of this, I want to weep on its behalf. On my behalf. My heart sinks, knowing all that comes after.

Because it was all so fragile. New and with its newness, so delicate. Easily crushed.

And if this book really is my mystery of faith, dedicated to going back over all of my steps and trying to figure out where I first lost it, what exactly happened to it, and whether or not I can find it again, this is also the point in my story where I almost find it. Early on in graduate school when everything was getting so exciting. Where the possibility of faith was right there at the tips of my fingers and I nearly had it, nearly allowed it air to breathe and room to occupy my heart and soul and space to grow. I can't help wondering what would have happened to this budding, maybe-faith, if all these other things hadn't also happened, too.

So, in this mystery story, what happens here in the arc of it now is this:

The priest-professor takes me and the delicate shell of faith nestled in my palms and crushes us both. When I ask for help from those above him, I accidentally call upon his closest cronies to come to his aid instead of mine. When they arrive to take in the damage he's sown upon me, instead of rescuing *me*, they rescue *him*. Then the Catholic Church and its hierarchy see what he's done and—as with everyone else their priests did something like this to—pour water right over the dust of that faith and me until it and I am completely washed away.

Until finally, here and now, I am reopening this cold case during a time when I have more power in my life, more confidence, more skill, more energy, and more of the will to do so, when I am revived enough to try and go back over my steps and see what happened at this very difficult juncture of my life. Where I finally feel ready to search for all the clues even in this place called graduate school where I swore I'd never return, where my faith was truly left for dead. To see if I can raise that faith up again. And isn't that resurrection?

19

Here come the other elephants.

One of the elephant(s) in the room right now is this: Why would I—why would any person—still long to be part of a religion, a tradition, a faith that has showed itself to be so corrupt, that has abused so many people, and that often operates like some kind of criminal organization? A tradition so sexist, it makes my head spin, so profoundly anti-LGBTQIA+ that it makes me want to scream a long, endless cry that never stops?

I don't. But I also do. And I also don't.

Over the years and a lot of despair, I've learned to step back to try and see the big picture of Catholicism. I've done this as a survival mechanism. This picture includes the kinds of horrors I listed prior. But when I take a big enough step back, I can see how there is the physical and the human, the worldly and the awful, the power-hungry, destructive force that can be a tradition, and then there are also the longings of the human heart for God, for hope, for Meaning. There is the love shown us by a community that cares. There are rituals and symbols and stories that hold the power to raise the dead. And while it's easy to turn away from the raging monster of a tradition, it's far less easy to turn away from the hunger of the soul and the people around you who open their arms and the need to somehow get through all the grief to something on the other side that looks like life again.

So despite how criminal and destructive a tradition may be, a soul still hungers. My soul still hungers. Both things can exist at the same time. They do inside of me. As I get older and life gets more beautiful in certain ways, and more painful and wounding in so many others, it becomes even clearer to me that my attempts to shake off this faith-thing have not worked. I have tried so hard to excise it from my brain and my body and my heart because it has harmed my person so deeply and in so many ways. But I can pretend all I want that I no longer care, that I refuse to care, that I do not need this tradition, this religion that so often disgusts me, *and yet I do.* Or I need *something.* I want faith in spite of everything, I deserve it, and we all do, don't we? Regardless of the bad and the ugly? I recognize this as true and maybe you do, too.

The question is, what does faith look like after we strip away the rest?

Is there anything left?

When I was a kid and enraged about something kids get upset about, like maybe a toy I wanted that my mother refused to buy for me, my mother would hand me a napkin. Or sometimes a piece of construction paper.

"Tear it up," she'd say.

I remember the first time she did this, and I looked up at her like, *What?*

She held a paper napkin out to me and said, "Rip this up into tiny pieces. Yell if you want while you do it. Afterwards, you're going to feel better."

My angry child's brow furrowed. But I took the napkin from her hand.

I ripped a corner of it. I ranted a little, side-eyeing my mother as I did.

"Keep going," she said.

So I did. I shredded that thing. I whined and complained and then my mother gave me another. I was tearing those napkins to pieces and they were going everywhere. Of course, afterward, my mother made me clean it all up. But it turned out she was right—I did feel better. Taking my anger out on those napkins helped me experience the anger and let it go. In fact, by the end of all that ripping and shredding, I was cracking up. So was my mother. We were both giggling. Grandma showed up to witness the ruckus in the kitchen and she was laughing, too. Crisis averted. Anger spent, relief followed.

The lesson?

It's okay to be angry, and it's important to let ourselves experience anger to then try and get past it. Or to live with it somehow. Anger is healthy and normal and human. It's good to get it out. But there are harmless ways to express our anger—say, by ripping up paper and napkins and tossing the pieces into the air. And there are harmful ways, too, often harmful to ourselves and to others in the process. We need to do our best to find productive ways to experience the rage we feel, otherwise it will eat us from the inside. I certainly know how rage can eat me from the inside. I have spent years with rage for the Catholic hierarchy and the hierarchy at my graduate institution and even the field of Catholic theology eating at my insides like some terrible, toxic force.

Obviously, the Catholic Church is not a pile of napkins I can rip to shreds, and the field of Catholic theology isn't, either. But it might be time for some proverbial shredding to see what relief might follow afterward. I want to stop the rage I harbor for this tradition and its counterparts, so it stops eating me from the inside like poison.

So I'm going to log a whole bunch of official complaints against the Catholic Church and see how I might get past them. There are too many to list them all, so I'll only try and get through the big ones. The biggest is from my grad school years, but now here come the rest.

Elephant 1

The first involves the lack of care or interest in young adults shown by the hierarchical Catholic Church.

Because there are so many wonderful evangelical Christians in my life, and because I've been immersed in evangelical communities in various ways on behalf of my research, I also know how many evangelicals idealize the high liturgical traditions of Catholicism. Some of you secretly or not so secretly may be jealous of them, wish for them in your own lives, and long to worship in our fancy Gothic churches with their stunning vaulted ceilings and their scent of incense wafting in the air. Maybe some of you would even trade your rockstar-level worship bands, all that Starbucks and the donuts and pastor-lectures on finances, for a few people dressed in flowing robes carrying jeweled staffs down the center aisle of a very solemn space for mass.

Well. There is a dark underbelly to all this pomp and circumstance.

The price? Young adult Catholics and their inclusion. In this very high-minded tradition, there is little effort to engage the younger person. It's not a big deal when you're a small child. There's Sunday school for kids. But as a child becomes a young adult, there's a widespread disregard for the life stuff that slams into teens upon reaching puberty. The Catholic tradition's answer to questions about sex and struggles in dating and relationships, is basically, No. No, no, no, and no. No or silence. No or let's pretend it's not there. One of the only books written for Catholic young adults on the topic of sex and relationships is penned by an older man who also basically says, *No, no, no, and no, and definitely no to being gay*, in a very sad imitation of something like *Every Young Man's Battle*. The whole situation is really embarrassing. Also pretty tragic, because young adulthood is a time when people could really use some meaningful conversation on these subjects.

I also know very well what a long-term disaster *I Kissed Dating Goodbye* has been for so many evangelical youth from Joshua Harris's generation. But the tradition that evangelicals have of empowering young adults and college grads to speak and write and lead on matters of faith? Even matters of faith and sex? We Catholics do not have it. But boy, do we need it.

Also, on social matters, and trying to reach young adults where they are on the subject of, say, even organizing a ski trip or a dance, or truly anything fun at all in a Catholic parish context? It's rare. Often when a diocese or local parish does try to actually organize such things, the response may be one of fear or admonishment from the local bishop. Because what if, I don't know, the topic of S-E-X arises on that trip? What if there are questions about S-E-X?! What if, *gulp*, someone brings a CONDOM! What if someone says the word "Condom!" The whole tradition might shatter in some cataclysmic disaster! This is the vibe, at least.

After talking to thousands of Catholic college students over the last twenty years, I'm not exaggerating when I say the Catholic Church's approach to young adults is one of abandonment. And then when young adults fall away from the tradition because it offers them next to nothing as they attempt to navigate the difficult seas of this time in their lives, the people in charge often wring their hands, wondering why they've all left. As though it isn't totally and completely obvious already.

One caveat. Catholic colleges and universities—save my graduate institution—can be pretty amazing in trying to repair some of this damage. But they, too, often operate as though the faith piece of their institution is off in some corner, everyone trying to avoid polluting the rest of campus life with Catholicism. There are not a lot of Walmart greeters for the tradition on a Catholic college campus. While I understand that the reasons for exiling the Catholic tradition to its own, unique corner of campus is out of respect for the diverse beliefs and backgrounds students bring to these same colleges, and that the spirit behind this effort is well meaning, the effect is to again not provide the social and spiritual network young adults need to keep their faith alive during these rocky years. And while there is opportunity to reconcile some of Catholicism's Big No's at these colleges, as well as the opportunity to worship and be social in a Catholic context, this also often occurs in a very sectioned-off part of campus life. So many, maybe even most students can get through their undergraduate careers not even knowing these opportunities are there.

Elephant 2

Then there are the many ways this tradition of my youth has not only abandoned and alienated but humiliated and condemned LGBTQIA+ people. There is much to say on this front, but I've said plenty about it elsewhere, and if I go too far into it here, I'll lose my way on everything else. I'll get too depressed to keep going. So, much like what I say above, I'll register that I find it despicable. As anti–social justice and anti–what Jesus would do and anti-Gospel as it gets. One day, I have faith that all Christian traditions, not just the Catholic one, will realize this gross injustice committed against all people who claim one of these identities. I have faith because I have to believe these traditions will get there. This or risk dying completely.

I also know that steps are being taken fairly across the board in most Christian traditions toward rectifying these injustices, to reinterpret the tradition and revelation toward the goal of inclusion, even within Catholicism. But they are so far too baby-in-size to make a real difference, in my opinion. There is such a long way to go.

So here is yet another big, supersized elephant. And I'm definitely with Nadia Bolz-Weber, Rachel Held Evans, and company all the way on this one.

Elephant 3

Confession: One of my favorite things about being invited to speak about my research on an evangelical college campus is getting to give a chapel talk. I love chapel talks. I enjoy them for many reasons, but one of the biggest is this: As a Catholic woman, it just feels so very transgressive. Like, I'm not supposed to be doing it. Like, this is me accidentally getting invited to break one of the cardinal rules of Catholicism (pun intended). I mean, do you evangelical people realize Catholic women aren't supposed to stand there at a pulpit? Even if it's technically not as a pastor? But still, to talk on matters related to faith? Did you realize that *my body specifically* isn't supposed to be fit to do these things because it's not male? That Catholics take this stuff quite literally, which is why there still aren't women priests?

When I am walking onto the stage to give one of these chapel talks, standing there as I'm introduced after the worship band has played their opening songs and someone has called us together in prayer, I always feel so sneaky. Like, I'm getting away with something women aren't supposed to. I adore the whole shebang. It makes me feel invited to the table, it makes me feel respected, I think of it as one of the greatest honors of my career to be offered this privilege, to stand up there and speak to the students and faculty within a cherished faith context on a campus.

Despite being a woman.

Which brings me to one of the big things that really burns me about so many varieties of Christianity, but especially Catholicism: women. Women's bodies, women's roles, the rejection and resistance to the feminine divine, what women are allowed to be and do and are not allowed to be and do, in general, but especially with respect to matters of faith. In contexts of faith. Christianity has a women problem when it comes to positions of authority, and Catholicism has one of the worst women problems of all. It's also true that, as a woman, I can be a professor of Catholic theology, which gives me a certain kind of authority to speak on matters of faith. But there are still plenty of limits. Way too many. And in my efforts to do this, I've collided with a few bishops and cardinals over the years because I'm a woman and a feminist, which I'll come back to later.

As with Elephant 2, I'm sure you already know the drill on this front, so I'll say no more. But it needed to be acknowledged. And it's another supersized one.

Elephant 4

The hierarchy of the Catholic Church loves to advertise all they're doing to make up for decades of criminal behavior and cover-ups related to the worldwide abuse crisis. Bishops and cardinals love to say they're holding "private" meetings with victims to bring about healing, and to try and restore the faith people once had in Catholicism as a tradition and institution. But the cover-up continues, the secrecy continues, and in my opinion, these efforts are just lip service.

It's also not just my opinion, it's my experience.

My graduate university, so brazenly called the Catholic University of America, once had as its chancellor Theodore McCarrick, the disgraced cardinal defrocked for abuse. He was actually chancellor during the time I came forward to ask for help. Because of the revelations about McCarrick, the university launched a flashy reconciliation project about the abuse crisis and reaching out to victims. But definitely not victims who were made victims on their campus.

Recently, I've taken steps toward asking for reconciliation with my graduate institution because of this public outreach. I've been put off, blown off, ignored, misled, had them attempt to reinforce my now-twenty-three-year-old NDA rather than engage with me in moving forward. It's been a terrible dance. I wish I didn't care, that I didn't want them to apologize, didn't want them to engage with me, but I do. I want them to try and help me heal this old, old wound. I want them to say they're sorry for what happened. I want them to admit that something did indeed happen and that it happened to me and that it cost me my future. I want them to release me from that NDA because it's the right thing to do. I want what happened to me in graduate school to finally feel like it's over. I want to no longer be the one to carry the shame of what this professor and priest did on my own shoulders. I want them to take this burden of secrecy back from me, and see what it's like to carry the consequences themselves.

I'm trying to forgive myself, too, for wanting these things.

There could be a much larger parade of elephants making their way across the chapters of this book. But these are the grandpas for me. The kind that have grown so big, sometimes I can't see around them. I've gotten used to climbing up high to try and see over their backs, or crouching down low to peer under their bellies, searching for just the right moment when I can scoot my way on through. This is me scooting on through right now.

20

God is in the lasagna.

When my mother was finally diagnosed with fourth-stage ovarian cancer, the treatment was brutal. One result of the chemo was that she didn't have the energy to cook. She was basically incapacitated. I worried how my father and grandma would eat without her at the helm, making meals, while I was away at grad school. I considered leaving my program to come home and cook for them. At this point my grandma was suffering from Alzheimer's.

I went home to visit after her initial surgery, and I remember sitting at the kitchen table trying to get some reading done for my classes. My overall plan was to cook and cook and cook during my weekend and stuff things into the freezer, plus teach my father how to heat everything up when I wasn't there. My position at the table had a view of the front entryway to the house.

The bell rang, my father answered the door.

It was someone from church. "How's Connie?"

Connie is my mother. I could hear the person asking about her from the kitchen, my father murmuring an answer I couldn't quite decipher. Some brief conversation ensued, the door shut, my father turned around, and in his hands was a large metal tray covered in aluminum foil.

"What's that?" I asked.

He stared down at it. "A lasagna?"

He carried it into the kitchen and set it down on the island. I joined him there, and we lifted up the corner of the foil. Yup, definitely a lasagna. Thick noodles covered in sauce with parmesan dotting the top. It was recently made and making my stomach grumble. "Who brought it?"

My father shook his head. "Someone your mother knows from church?"

He hadn't gotten their name. I think my father was still too dazed from all that was happening with my mother to ask.

"That was really nice of them to bring food," I said.

I covered the lasagna back up and put it into the fridge.

Not long afterward, the bell rang again. My father answered again. He again came back into the kitchen with a lasagna. This proceeded to occur throughout the weekend. The bell would ring, we'd open the door to find yet another parishioner bearing a foil tray or large Pyrex baking dish of something or other, often involving red sauce and pasta. Sometimes it took the form of baked ziti, occasionally there would be a traditional casserole, but more often than not, it was a layered, cheesy, steamy lasagna, perhaps with spinach instead of meat. A few of the people who showed up were from my mother's school, but most of them were also members of the local parish where my family had attended mass since we moved to Narragansett. In addition to people showing up with food, nuns and priests from our parish were showing up, too, to check in on my mother and to offer her communion. One after the other, people arrived with one form of nourishment or another, be it practical and very human, or more divine in nature. Both forms equally necessary.

Our fridge was soon stuffed and overflowing. There were now trays and dishes sitting on the countertops. It was like the loaves and the fishes but the tomato sauce and ricotta cheese edition.

My dad was wide-eyed about how to handle so much food.

But me? I was beyond grateful. I was in awe. It seemed like magic that these people—without anyone asking them to do this—anticipated exactly what my family would need in the coming weeks and months, and also somehow anticipated that the only remaining working chef of the family (i.e., me) was trying to get through grad school an eight-hour drive away. So they went and provided exactly what we needed. For me, for us. For my mother. I know what I've said before about prayer and how I just don't buy it. But if there is such a thing as prayer and getting prayers you didn't realize you needed to utter answered before you can think to utter them, this would be one of those occasions.

"What are we going to do with all of this?" my father asked, taking in the buffet of baking dishes and foil trays all over our kitchen.

With a smile, I turned to my dad and patted him on the shoulder. "We're going to freeze everything. And then I'm going to teach you how to heat it up when I'm not around."

For the rest of the weekend, I cut up lasagnas into serving-size squares, wrapped them individually, and arranged them in the freezer block by block. The same with the baked ziti. I thought a lot about the bounty that had befallen my family in our time of tragedy.

As it turns out, the Catholic Church may be full of corruption and hypocrisy, but the Church is also full of people. Good, caring, generous of heart people. The Church is a community, the Church is the Body of Christ and sometimes the people of the Church actually live out what Catholics believe about the Eucharist—that if a part of the Body of Christ is sick, we are meant to work to heal it. My mother was part of that Body. So was my family. She needed healing and we did, too, by proxy. Our Catholic parish showed up in force to heal whatever part they could.

If I was daring enough to count myself a person of faith without any of the caveats I always come up with to stop from counting myself this way, if I can somehow forget those giant-size elephants, I can begin to see all those doorbell ringers bearing gifts of steaming ricotta and melty mozzarella and sausage and meatballs and occasionally spinach as a whole parade of well-meaning, local, culinary Jesuses. Right?

While we're discussing the God of oozy mozzarella and the people who show up when we are down, and how the Catholic Church may indeed behave in reprehensible ways, when meanwhile its average parishioners can make someone like me believe that God is showing up at the door of my house in Rhode Island, I want to make an important differentiation. One I often hang on to.

In graduate school, the professor who talked to me about Heidegger on my first day also talked often about the difference between the Big C Church and the little c church. The Big C Church is the one we tend to default to when we are speaking about the Catholic tradition. You know, the pope, the cardinals, the bishops, the hierarchy. The people in charge, the people with power, the people who can make us feel disempowered in relation to them, like we have no role or voice within this faith.

But the small c church? Well, it's made up of people.

Everyday, ordinary people who go to mass on Sundays, who attend school with you as you grow up, your friends and neighbors and teachers and the people you run into at the beach during summer if you live in Rhode Island like I did. They may lead a song or two during church, they may teach Sunday school or even be a eucharistic minister, but they may just be the average grandma next to you in the pew. The family you shake hands with during the sign of peace at mass. Someone who smiles from across the sanctuary when you catch each other's eyes, someone who hands you a tissue when they see tears running down your face. The ordinary priests who show up for a parish despite the terrible things their bosses have done, trying to do the best they can to be there for the people on the ground who are hurting or who've lost their faith. The very human people of God.

The small c church is also the church that shows up at a family's door when someone who lives inside is going through chemo and can't get out of bed. The small c church is the one who cooks for that family when they're in need and shows the face of God in bubbling, cheesy pasta with red sauce.

The small c church appeared to me and my family as a parade of lasagnas. As an offering of warm, homemade food that would nourish our souls as much as our stomachs and our bodies. The small c church is the one that often does far more to help someone hang on to a faith tradition than all the popes and cardinals in all their formal proclamations and ceremonies together across all of history. And the small c church so often does this armed with only a wooden spoon, some cans of tomatoes, a dash of oregano, and a whole lot of good intentions.

Another thing I will never forget is what the teachers at my mother's Catholic elementary school did after her diagnosis, and that subsequent rush to the hospital so she could undergo major surgery.

My mother was beloved at her school among the teachers, the parents of kids, the kids themselves. She worked at that school for decades, and it seemed she somehow taught all the children of Rhode Island at one point or another. Her diagnosis arrived right when school was about to start again at the end of August. It was immediately clear she would miss many months, if not the entire academic year.

Would my mother need to quit teaching? My mother's job provided the family's health insurance, and there'd be no affording the health care she needed to fight the cancer if she couldn't work. We were scared. We had no idea what to do.

Well. The teachers at my mother's school knew. They got together one day and discussed my mother's situation and decided to pool their sick days to get my mother through the whole school year and keep her job. I don't know who informed my mother that her colleagues decided to do this—I wasn't there. But I remember when she told me about their plan.

The phone in my DC apartment rang. I answered.

"Things at school are going to be okay," my mother said.

"What do you mean?"

"The other teachers donated their sick days to me."

"What?"

"They pooled them and gave them to me. So I won't lose my job or the insurance."

I tried to take this in. "Wow," was all I came up with.

"I know," my mother said.

"I didn't even realize you could do that," I said.

"I didn't, either, sweetheart."

Yet another prayer answered, one we didn't know to utter. But somehow, our wonderful community and parish anticipated what we needed on our behalf without us needing to ask. It seemed like a miracle. The small c church swooped in to save the day again.

One big reason I still care about this Catholic tradition that has hurt me and so many others so deeply are things like the lasagna. All those lasagnas and casseroles and trays of baked ziti when my mother was sick. All those caring people who came to our door and offered genuine consolation and home cooking as a means of showing us love and care during a time when my family needed it most. People we didn't even know, not really, but who'd seen my mother at church and heard about her diagnosis and surgery and treatment and the hard road we had ahead of us; who knew about my grandmother's Alzheimer's and that my mother was her primary caretaker. Nice people who were part of our Catholic parish who wanted to do something, so they showed up at our door with food. Nice people who included ordinary nuns and local priests who came to sit with my mother on the couch, to offer her the Eucharist because it was important to her and they knew this and they cared.

And those sick days. They were grace amid the devastation. They felt like—and they quite literally functioned as—our salvation. For better or worse, when and where else do things like this happen but in a church community?

My mother, my father, my grandmother, and I—we all survived on these gestures. They offered us nourishment for the body in so many ways, but more than this, they offered nourishment for our souls. They reminded us that we weren't alone in this. That it wasn't only on us to make it through this time, step by step, day by day, that there were many other people in step along with us. That they were willing to carry us through if we got too tired and overwhelmed to carry ourselves. That they would feed us when we were hungry with the work of their own hands.

You know how people say that God is in the details? I have often thought that if there is a God, then God was definitely in all of those lasagnas. That at the time of my mother's cancer, God was in the ricotta and the oozy mozzarella and the store-bought noodles layered between them. That during those months when my mother was first receiving treatment, God took the form of sausage and meatballs and big pots of tomato sauce, and God was in those sick days offered by my mother's colleagues. God was in the answered prayers that we didn't need to utter because the parish community got there first so we didn't have to pray for those things at all.

So the Big C Church can be a reprehensible body while at the same time the small c church can be a nourishing body. And the Catholic tradition may make me want to scream in rage, but it's also true that so many Catholic people and communities have made me want to weep with gratitude. Both things are true at once. The Big C and the small c coexist together. And that is the tricky thing, isn't it?

21

This is what a Catholic looks like.

"If the Catholic Church was a big house with a yard," I am telling a group of young women students sitting in a classroom before me, "then sometimes I am on the porch lying in a hammock, and at others I'm in the street right along the edge of that yard, protesting. Or heckling."

My students start laughing.

I've made it through graduate school, made it out of the place where this priest nearly ruined my life. At this moment, I believe I made it out clean. I didn't, but I don't know this yet. I'm still kidding myself that I'm okay. I've gotten an academic job at a small Catholic college in Vermont that I soon leave because of my awful male colleagues who don't want a woman in theology, who use the grief over my mother's death to critique everything about me, including the lack of a smile on my face when I walk the halls. But I do love my students. They are the best part.

The classroom where I teach is drab, gray, fluorescently lit, with barely a window, an ugly gray floor, tiles, everything sterile, glaring. The course is Women and Spirituality. We often rearrange the desks so we can sit in a circle. I love the contrast of my students and the wild outfits they sometimes wear to class to the dull decor, the contrast of their loud laughter and the humor they hand out freely during our meetings that brings this drab place to life with so much humanity. I enjoy matching their open emotion with my own. I learn to be honest about myself with them, and when I tell them where I see myself in relation to Catholicism, it's one of these honest moments. We talk so much about creating safe spaces for students, but sometimes they create safe spaces for teachers to be ourselves.

"But, Professor Freitas," one woman says, "how can *you* call yourself Catholic?"

"What do you mean?" I ask her back. I really don't understand.

"Well, you know..." She gestures her chin at me, Exhibit A.

I am wearing jeans and tall, spiky heels, paired with one of my favorite T-shirts from the early aughts. It's black, fitted, and says in big, fiery, hot-pink letters, "This is what a feminist looks like." Courtesy of Ashley Judd. I liked that T-shirt's statement, its loudness, its pinkness, its femininity, and in its femininity its wholehearted defiance. By now I've learned to use certain outfits like weapons, and why not? The Catholic hierarchy does, and didn't we so recently have a pope famous for his special-ordered red Gucci shoes? How I dress has always been a public statement of self—a hanging on to myself.

But when these young women ask, *Who do I think I am, calling myself Catholic?* I realize something important. The answer is significant and life-changing.

These young women are struggling to identify themselves as Catholic. They just can't see themselves as Catholic. Like, literally they can't. When they look in the mirror, when they think about how they live and socialize, it doesn't "look" Catholic, at least not how they've learned to understand what Catholicism looks like.

First, they are women. Second, they are women college students immersed in a culture of hooking up and typical college hedonism. Third, like I said, the Catholic Church says pretty much nothing of direct value to young adults as they try and swim in the very complicated waters of youth, especially during college. Most of the people around them who identify as Catholic are either their parents (from whom they feel very different), or a bunch of old celibate men. Occasionally nuns (also celibate). In other words: young women Catholic role models in whom they can see themselves as Catholic are few and far between.

What I should have done (even though this is dorky) is have a T-shirt made for all of us that said, in hot-pink defiant lettering, "This is what a feminist Catholic looks like." YEAH!

This is yet another place where Catholics are so different from evangelicals, with all the worship bands and opportunities to be lead singers or be important to your community from the time you are a teenager. Young women can write books that show how to be a role model to other young women. You can do so in hot-pink high heels. Or your favorite sundress. Or soccer gear. Even if you disagree with evangelical culture and the role models and leaders within it, *it's still there*. You can literally see what this looks like all over. Young adults cropping up and speaking out, maybe some of them look like you, or the you that you'd like to be. There is a lack of diversity in what it looks like to be a woman within evangelical culture, and youth culture specifically. But at least there is *something*.

In Catholicism, we have none of this. I mean, we've got the Virgin Mary. And *The Sound of Music*. But that only goes so far. Mainly we've got an absence of models, especially young women models. Which is another reason staying Catholic is so damn hard, and one of the reasons so many young adults leave the tradition as they grow into adulthood. We can't see ourselves represented in this tradition led mostly by old celibate men, so we conclude there is no place for us. There is no one like us, so we skedaddle.

So there I am, standing in a classroom full of young women assessing my outfit and me. Its Catholic-ness. My Catholic-ness. Waiting for my answer about why I'm calling myself Catholic.

You might be thinking: *You're not the best Catholic role model for these young women.* And I get it. It's complicated. I'm complicated. But I've worked hard on behalf of this faith business, however imperfectly. My relationship to Catholicism has survived significant challenges over the years. And there I am, still sticking this out, trying to make it work. Which makes me like every other human trying to do the same thing in their own very imperfect traditions, in their own very imperfect ways.

I decide to just go for it.

"Of course someone like me can be Catholic," I tell those young women. I point to my T-shirt and its words. "And still wear this statement about feminism. And put on these jeans in the morning. And walk in these high heels. And talk of the divine feminine. And just, well, be me."

As the students' eyes are on me, I realize that whatever I do next is crucial. They are searching to call themselves Catholic, too, and for some reason they identify with me, see something of themselves in me, someone who shows them that even in all their college struggles, their femininity, and let's be honest, their sexuality, they can swim through those college waters and still be Catholic. If I call myself Catholic, then maybe they also can call themselves Catholic.

This is also the moment I understand what it means to be a witness.

I am the witness. For better or worse.

"I *am* Catholic," I tell them, once and for all. "And just because I don't look like some of the other Catholics in your life, or just because I show myself to have different views on morality than the traditional ones you're used to hearing, or just because I dress this way and laugh loudly like you do, doesn't mean there isn't room for people like me in this tradition. Or room for people like you. There *is* room for you in this tradition. All of you. I made room for myself and I'm not giving it up. You can make room, too. Because there is room for all of us."

Surprised faces blink at me, some of them nodding. I can see these women considering what I've said, and thinking hard. I will never forget this moment. It changes how I speak about myself.

After this, among students, I begin identifying as Catholic before I'm asked, especially with groups of young women. I realize how badly young women Catholics need to see some young-ish women Catholics to find their own place in the tradition, or to try. I realize, too, how badly I need this. We all need lots of different kinds of women for this, and I am only one example, and like my students, I need examples of my own. Yet if I can be one example of one of the women they might need, then I surely will be. Even if it means a whole bunch of bishops rolling in their graves and also making the rest of the men in my department at the time extremely twitchy.

Maybe it seems a little weird to call myself Catholic given how the jury is still out—kind of way, way out—on the belief front for me. I mean, I did say at the start of this chapter that if the Catholic Church was a big house with a yard, I'm either outside in a hammock or in the street protesting. But the small c church people who raised me, the nuns on the beach and the parishioners with their lasagnas and the caroling neighbors and of course my parents and grandma, gave this tradition to me as best as they could. The Italian side of its culture. So it is, technically, mine. Also, maybe fake it till you make it? But I'm pretty sure that if my mother could have heard me that day in my classroom, she would have laughed in that, *I've got you* sort of way. Nodding her head, narrowing her eyes, and saying, *I told you so, Donna Marie Angelina.* You *are what a Catholic looks like. I knew it all along.*

Speaking of bishops rolling in graves and the Big C Church, I can add cardinals to the list of people who get twitchy when I call myself Catholic because I'm a feminist and I also write about sex and faith. My run-ins with the Catholic hierarchy over the years are so absurd that if they weren't awful, they'd be hilarious. Because while I told those young women there was room for them in the Catholic tradition, just like there is room for me, not everybody agrees with me on that statement.

One day, I was sitting in my office in Boston, at the university where I landed a professor job after I left the small Catholic college in Vermont. My office was this weird little attic room with sloping ceilings. Visitors had to duck and stoop as they moved around, so as not to clock their heads. I was at my desk, working, surrounded by piles of papers and books. We're talking enormous stacks of books. People would send me so many books for review that towers of them rose and teetered like city blocks on the floor, the shelves, the furniture, any surface I could find.

My office phone rang. I picked it up. "Hello?"

"Is this Donna Freitas?" a man asked.

"Yes. Who is this?"

"This is the cardinal's office calling."

"Who?"

"The cardinal's office in Boston?"

Inside, I was thinking, *Like, the cardinal-cardinal?*

Like, a cardinal of the Catholic Church?

Like, The Actual Boston Cardinal?

Is this a prank?

At the time, the cardinal in Boston was Cardinal O'Malley. He is currently still one of the most powerful men in the hierarchy of the American Catholic Church.

I was immediately suspicious that someone from the cardinal's office was calling me. By then I'd published a book on my research about sex and faith during college, and was frequently invited to speak about my research. A few of these invitations led to run-ins with bishops and none of these run-ins were positive. They involved me eventually being disinvited to speak. One bishop went so far as to label me and my research dangerous.

A major feature of getting dinged by a bishop, I soon learned, was secrecy. Whoever won the honor of informing me that my invitation to speak had been rescinded had also typically been told by the bishop's office they were not allowed to tell me why. They were only allowed to say I was not allowed to speak on their diocesan property. But usually, the people who called were upset themselves—on my behalf, on their school or organization's behalf, on Catholicism's behalf. Our conversations would often include statements like, *I'm not supposed to tell you this, but the bishop doesn't want you to speak because of X.* Then they would tell me the basics of the problem.

The bishop found out you were a feminist.

Someone in the diocese saw online you were a feminist and called the bishop.

Your openness to LGBTQIA+ relationships is a problem.

Your work on sex and young adults is a problem.

One time, the person who called to say I was disinvited was so angry, she read the entire letter from the bishop about me word for word over the phone—this was the bishop who said I was dangerous. The woman prefaced this by explaining she'd been explicitly prohibited from telling me why my invitation was withdrawn. We had a good laugh about the letter, especially the parts about how I and my research were "dangerous" to Catholic youth, that I was "disobedient" and therefore "unfit" to stand before Catholics and call myself Catholic. Dangerous, disobedient, unfit, that's me. It did crack me up. But it also hurt. And it made me mad.

Whenever this happens, I always want to scream back at these men: *Do you know what one of your kind did to me when I was in graduate school? Don't you see how hard I am trying to stay in this tradition, how hard I am trying to forgive you all for what you've done, how you've treated me? Don't you realize that I am working to give other young adults the space and conversations they need to try and make their way through this whole Catholic situation as they grow up? What would you say if I told you I am one of the people who got covered up in that abuse scandal of yours? Would you be so quick to chastise me, to disinvite me, to piss me off?* These thoughts and questions scroll through me like poison. It's hard not to let these men get the better of me. But now back to this man calling me on behalf of the cardinal of Boston and wanting to talk.

Phone cradled between my ear and my shoulder, I swiveled around in my office chair to face the city of books, imagining that most of them would be considered heretical by the man on the other end of the line. So many were about sex and feminism, girls and women, the feminine divine. "Why is the cardinal's office calling me?" I asked the man. "Who is this anyway?"

"My name is Father B. I am the cardinal's secretary."

"And what it this about?"

"Well," he said, "I wanted to talk to you about LA Congress."

LA Congress is the biggest Catholic youth conference in the world, or it used to be, to the tune of forty thousand attendees. That year, I was to be one of the keynote speakers, invited to talk about my research on sex, spirituality, religion, and college students. It was a big deal. A huge deal. I was very excited about it and looking forward to the opportunity.

"What about LA Congress?"

Father B. hesitated. "We just want to make sure you know it was the LA cardinal who made the decision."

"And what decision is this?"

"Oh. No one has told you yet?"

"Told me *what?*"

"You should call the LA Congress people so *they* can tell you."

"Again, tell me *what?*"

My question was now met with silence.

Then finally, "The invitation for you to speak has been withdrawn."

Picture me, filling with dismay and rage. "What? Why?"

Father B. went on to equivocate, insist I needed to ask the nun in charge of speakers for this information, and to reassure me that the letter rescinding my invitation originated from a late-night "fax" sent by the LA cardinal's office to the Boston cardinal's office; but that Cardinal O'Malley's office was the office forced to act because I was a professor in Boston, which was in their neck of the woods.

At this point, I got very upset. I spoke briefly to the cardinal's secretary about what happened in graduate school, how experiences like this did not help me to forgive or forget and move forward. Then finally I wondered out loud to the man, "If you need *me* to call LA Congress to have them tell me I'm disinvited, why are you calling me now? What do you want from me?"

More silence and hesitation. Then, the truth. "We wondered if you were going to write about this?" By then I'd not only published a book about sex and faith during college, but I'd also been publishing lots of opinion pieces and articles in major, national newspapers and magazines about this topic. "We were hoping that you wouldn't," he went on.

It's almost like I'm in a comedic play. It's too absurd to make up.

The conversation with Father B. went further downhill from here. There were many subsequent conversations with him and others—me to the LA Congress office, the Boston cardinal's office to me, continuing to ask whether I would tell anybody what was going on, pointing the finger back at Cardinal Mahoney in LA as the real culprit behind the withdrawal of my invitation. The poor nun working at the conference was left to cryptically tell me it was my work on sex and young adults that was behind the disinvitation. When I pointed out this was the same work that got me invited to speak, she remained silent, as though to communicate, *I don't make the crazy rules in this place, but it's my job to follow them, big sigh.*

The Big C Church makes it really difficult to want to say I'm Catholic in public. But once I come down from the rage and pain provoked by such absurd behavior, I try to remember why I am still here and apply that label to myself. The small c church and all those lasagnas and sick days. The young women in my classroom whom I've taught and spoken to over the years. My mother, the amazing Catholic Walmart greeter. My grandma and my dad, who lovingly passed on the tradition. The scholar-nun, one of my academic idols, who invited me to her office to discuss what had happened with the cardinals. She made me tea, then told me this had happened to her with the hierarchy, too, more than once, that it had happened to so many other women whose books I've read and whose work I cherish and whom I could now count myself among; that I should be proud of this distinction. That these men would rather have me gone, which is exactly why I should definitely not go and give them the satisfaction of my leaving this Church.

"This is how you know your work matters," she told me that day. "That you are making a difference."

Not long after this, I found myself identifying openly, explicitly, defiantly as Catholic, in a very Catholic setting, at a prestigious Catholic university. Doing it on purpose. Doing it as rebellion.

There were a lot of college students in the audience. Lots of faculty, too, and plenty of Catholics from the local community. They expressly came to hear about the research on sex and hooking up and young adults that has made me dangerous and disobedient according to certain bishops and apparently a couple of cardinals. When I publicly called myself a Catholic and a Catholic theologian at this event, I was doing it for the students, but I was also doing it for me, maybe to prove something to myself. That I get to do this, that I deserve to do this, that this identity is mine and no one can take it from me, not even a pair of ridiculous cardinals. I also did it because I was standing on that stage, talking about sex. And I realized that it's important for someone who's comfortable talking about sex to call herself Catholic.

As I gave my lecture that evening at this prestigious Catholic university, where everyone was aware of my PhD and my research about young adults, I became aware of something else.

Here lies *my* power within Catholicism. My power in relation to the hierarchy. I was *embodying* it in public by doing what I was doing—just like that Catholic scholar-nun told me that day in her office. I suddenly understood what she meant.

Me calling myself Catholic in public is powerful. The power lies in my not leaving the tradition. In my staying, in publicly naming myself as Catholic, in claiming that title and still remaining myself in the process—myself, which involves being a woman who dresses the way I do, who is unafraid to speak her mind, and who is totally unafraid to talk about third-rail issues like sex in a Catholic setting or in any Christian setting, for that matter. Regardless of the abuse crisis and its corresponding cover-up of me by the Big C powers that are, I still earned my PhD and I earned it from the Catholic University of America. So I was going to straighten my theologian's hat and raise my eyebrows and look everybody in the face without blinking and claim my place in this tradition and claim my power to speak on behalf of it.

A challenge to some.

An offer to others: *I see you.*

We can all fit in this tent, you know.

If there's room for me, then maybe there's room for you, too.

Let's clear space for one another, okay?

Sometimes I imagine my mother's eyes going wide as I do this, and do so speaking about sex.

A little scandalized. A lot cringey perhaps.

Thinking, *Sex? Not my daughter!*

But I just smile and shrug back and trust she will love me regardless.

22

Citizen of the Catholic Church.

Eventually, I start to imagine myself in a tug-of-war: with me and my PhD and my research on one side, the whole Big C Church on the other. The bishops and the cardinals and even the pope. Team Hierarchy is pulling hard, sandaled feet dug in, jeweled attire sparkling with all of its riches, and they're trying to take this tradition away from me. Sometimes the people on the other side of the rope include the Catholic theologians to whom I can't tell my secret about grad school, and who've shown they don't really want to know it anyway. There are a few instances when I ask for help and people close their ears, turn away, and I am shamed about grad school and that priest all over again.

Despite the efforts to loosen my grip on this tradition, I have ghosts on my side. My grandmother, my father. My professor-mentor joins them there and he was a monsignor, so I've got a little hierarchical power pulling for me. But then my team's anchor arrives and it's my mother, a Catholic heavy-hitter. So I yank harder and harder, propelled by the strength of the people I love. Some of the time, I manage to hang on to my Catholicism in the face of all this bullshit—at least in public. But much of the time I find myself sitting in a pile of rubble.

While I may find rebellion in calling myself a Catholic in public, and relish this defiance, doing so doesn't heal the wounds of my own heart. The harm and the hurt and the burden of secrecy, of NDAs signed in desperation, of people who turned away rather than helped when I needed it. So in private, sometimes labeling myself Catholic feels wrong. Empty. Its own kind of Dark Night. The rubble piles so high, it covers me up, and isn't that the point of making people like me sign NDAs about abuse? To put us in positions where we can't see beyond the damage and we give up? That we are too overwhelmed to try?

Good thing I spent so much time with my dad playing with Legos. That he taught me to build.

The list of reasons the Big C Church rejects me grows longer with each passing year:

I call myself a feminist.

My work is on sex and faith, and I don't tell unmarried people not to have sex.

I'm pro LBTQIA+ and don't hide this.

I don't back down in the face of bishops who've disinvited me to speak.

My work is on sex and faith—period. And sex is scary.

I'm a woman. Catholic women with PhDs are scary.

I am an abuse victim. The hierarchy is very afraid of us. We are the scariest of all. And when, as an abuse victim, I ask for reconciliation and to be released from my NDA because it's the right thing for my Catholic university to do, they have a very hard time doing that right thing. They have a very hard time talking to me at all.

The list of reasons I refuse to be rejected by this tradition is shorter, more slippery, but I try to hang on anyway:

I am a feminist, and feminism taught me to reclaim things as my own.

I am pro-LGBTQIA+, and the tradition needs people like me to stay.

I can do more damage (so to speak) from within, like that scholar-nun told me.

I want to be a thorn in the side of these people.

I remember how the young women I meet are surprised when I call myself Catholic.

I deserve reconciliation from the powers in the Church who hurt and silenced me.

The way I've come to look at Catholicism and me is this: The Catholic Church is kind of like the United States government, Congress, the president. Often there are a whole bunch of people in power whom I would never want in power, for whom I would never vote, and yet I remain a citizen. I don't give up the country of my birth because people elect a president I can't stand. Part of living in a democracy like the United States is accepting this as reality.

Of course, the problem with this analogy is that the Catholic Church is not a democracy, and its people don't have any role or right to elect its leaders. The people who do have a vote in electing officials like the pope aren't elected themselves. Instead, they rise to power like in a dictatorship. It's also true there is yet to be a person in Catholic office who makes me feel truly hopeful, at least not during my lifetime so far. Pope Francis is better than Pope Benedict, sure, but he's definitely not good enough when it comes to leading this tradition through the crisis it sparked within itself by covering up decades of criminal activity within its priestly ranks.

I realize I'm not making the best case for this analogy of citizenship.

Sometimes I believe I'm simply done with Catholic theology and Catholicism, too. That there is more harm than good. That it is poisonous in the long run, because I've been so poisoned by it. And because of the Christian traditions' tendencies to hurt their followers (and their nonfollowers) in so many ways—for being women, for example, or for being women who don't have children, or for being gay, lesbian, transgender, nonbinary. For following the Bible this way and not that way, for understanding Jesus this way but not that way, for picking and choosing what to believe and what not to believe. For being imperfect, for having sex, for being human in general, for holding certain opinions and not others, for their politics, for their doubts, for their divorces and their abortions, and for their questioning of religious authorities in some way, shape, or form. For having been abused and wanting their abusers and the protectors of those abusers to own what they've done and to apologize for it with sincerity. To show real contrition for the harm.

Yet, despite how church leadership has failed me and so many fellow Catholics, Catholicism is still a very big tent. A small c tent where my mother found shelter and hope, where so many other Catholics, including priests and nuns, were positive forces in my childhood, my young adulthood, my education, and how I've become who I am. So I can't just seem to abandon it outright. And as much as I am acutely aware of the terrible, there is also a beauty in its history, its theology and symbols and rituals, and especially its people, so many loved ones who believe in it and who've worked over the course of their lives to do good in this world on behalf of it. So here I am still, one foot in, one foot out. Sometimes on the porch in a hammock and sometimes on the edge of the yard, debating whether I should step back onto the lawn again or if I should run the other way as fast as I can manage. But I'm definitely hanging on to my passport for now.

Then again, it's also true that I'm open to dual citizenship.

But there is a difference between identifying as Catholic in name and profession and being a person of faith. If you are a person of faith, you know exactly what I'm talking about. There are plenty of people who go through the motions of their tradition who don't really feel it in their hearts and souls and bodies. Who either don't care enough or who get stuck in the darkness like I do. When I think of the ways I'm a Catholic now, I suppose they seem fitting: like I've agreed to wear the fancy robes, the shiny trappings, but underneath, there's a hollowness.

It's also true that the trappings of my mother's Catholicism were rich and beautiful and I recognize them for what they are now— rituals with meaning, rituals that filled my tummy with ravioli on Sunday afternoons after church and that nourished my child's body with talk among members of my family as we enjoyed the cooking done by her and my grandmother's own hands. These rituals and symbols and trappings of Catholicism that also populated my world with invisible men and women we could talk to when we needed help and hope, the saints always ready to hear us crying out. Catholicism was a world and culture for my mother that was real and vibrant, filled with nuns at our kitchen table and little children singing in schools and time taken among family and giving out plates of cookies to all the neighbors and angels in the backseat of cars saving husbands and fathers from sure death and people we don't even know very well showing up with divine lasagnas and trays of baked ziti and daily communion on the couch.

Which is not hollow at all. I can see this with my own eyes now, too. I am no longer blind to it, like I used to be. But my mother *felt* it. So deeply. She had faith.

I want to feel it. Deep in my heart, my soul, my body.

Whether it's Catholic or not, I want the faith piece to be real to me. But I can't seem to let myself have it where it truly counts.

23

The faith of my mother.

There is a beautiful Catholic church across the street from where I live in Brooklyn. One day, somewhere during the time of the silly cardinals and bishops and not long before my divorce, I crossed the street and walked through its doors for mass on a Sunday morning. I don't know what possessed me. I hadn't been to mass in years. It's sometimes easier to kick dirt over the whispers of your heart that wish for God, to try and muffle the sounds of it.

But on that morning, I walked straight down the center aisle and slid across to the end of one of the pews, in case I needed to make a run for it during the service. When a man showed up wanting to sit in the same row, I got up so he could scoot inside. I wasn't giving up my escape route for anybody.

The priest arrived and the mass began.

I stood up, I sat down, I knelt, the memory of these movements rote, written into my muscles, robotic. I didn't need to think, it's just what happens when I am at a mass.

I remember seeing the Tony Award–winning play *Doubt* on Broadway, which takes up the abuse scandal, starring Brian O'Byrne in the role of Father Flynn, played by Philip Seymour Hoffman in the movie adaptation. I was sitting up front in the theater, maybe in the second row. The play starts with a monologue that is really a homily, with the priest standing at the edge of the stage in the center. He talks to the audience like he's speaking to a congregation on a Sunday. I was so captivated by Brian O'Byrne that night, I forgot he was an actor and that I was not in a church at mass on a Sunday. When he finished the homily and did the sign of the cross, and spoke the words that accompany this ritual, *In the name of the Father, the Son, and the Holy Spirit,* I did the sign of the cross with him automatically, because that is what my body knows to do in such a situation. I'd forgotten I was in a theater, that Father Flynn wasn't a real priest, that he was an actor reciting the lines of a play. I wasn't alone, either. So many people around me did the very same thing, crossing themselves, murmuring the words. We glanced around at each other as we realized what we'd done, chuckling nervously about our reactions.

On the day I walked into that church in Brooklyn, I have no memory of what the priest talked about for the homily, or what scripture the priest discussed. I can barely remember what the priest looked like at the altar up front, and he certainly wasn't as captivating as Brian O'Byrne or Philip Seymour Hoffman. But in the end, none of this mattered.

What I do remember is far more important:

The presence of my mother and my grandmother in that church.

While I was murmuring the words of the prayers I've said since I was a small child.

In the gestures of the service, the standing, the sitting, the kneeling.

In the voices of the people singing the hymns around me.

In the echoes of the saints all over the church in the paintings and the statues.

In the sculpture of Mary up front.

Suddenly my mother and my grandmother were with me again, these two women who taught me these prayers and songs and the flow of the mass and when to stand and kneel and sit and why to care about the saints and Mary.

This is the beauty of a tradition and its rituals, isn't it? There is power in their repetition on every Sunday of a child's life, how it seeps into our bones and our brains and our very bodies as muscle memory. They can raise the dead through prayers and songs and words and bodily gestures, allowing us time with our loved ones in the midst of our deepest grief and loss and despair. These rituals and traditions hold the power to give me back my mother and my grandmother for an hour. And what a power that is.

I sat there, tears rolling down my cheeks, palms pressed flat on the wood of the pew, my head tilted toward the vaulted ceiling, eyes closed. I let myself feel my mother and my grandmother there with me, l let myself *believe* they were there with me. I didn't care if this was true or real, those doubting words never entered my head. They were irrelevant. At least for a while.

On that Sunday, something shifted, a knock, a bump in my heart, something real moving in my body. For the first time maybe in my whole life, the mass held real power, a precious power. I suddenly knew this was the reason we have liturgy, the hierarchy be damned. A faith tradition holds the power to raise the dead so we can make it one more day in our lives, so we can feel heartened enough to go on amid the eternal wounding of being human. So we don't feel wholly alone even when we are very alone.

I looked around the church and saw all the people who were there—many of them old, few who were young, but there were families and there were men and women sitting alone, and there were clearly the rich and also the poor, and then there was me, among them. If I was there, then surely at least one other person—maybe even many people—also regularly sparred with doubt like I do, but come to church anyway and feel some consolation. We were all there together, in our beliefs and also our doubts. And if my mother and my grandmother indeed showed up for me that morning, then how many others of the dead were there, too, to console and comfort the living who sat beside me? How many people I couldn't see but who had come for those who needed them during the mass? And isn't this what the communion of saints is all about? Isn't this why my mother wanted this tradition to be my own during my whole childhood and adult life?

All of these thoughts and feelings swirled inside me.

The mass ended.

I walked out of the church with everyone else.

I crossed the street back to my Brooklyn apartment.

I was filled with doubt again.

I am perpetually caught between two churches: the one my family gave me, the one my mother wanted for me so badly, and the corrupt force the Catholic Church can be in this world and that it's been to me specifically. I am caught between the nuns on the beach and the boys in the pews and the loving of Jesus as a child, the delicious raviolis on Sunday afternoons and the Bible stories with my dad and that joyful singing as my mother cooked in the kitchen, versus the bishops and the cardinals and the abuse and the rejection and the condemnation of so many people for being who they are and loving who they love and even for having been abused by a priest. I am caught between beautiful memories of the past and my more current experiences of being disinvited by bishops and cardinals. Between the love my mother shared and handed down to me, as a way of saving her own daughter, and the rejection I often feel amid Catholic theologians and in Catholic hierarchical situations. In the way the Big C Church has refused my overtures for reconciliation, who replies to me with lawyers wielding my NDA rather than sitting down face-to-face and talking like the humans that we are.

But then sometimes I start laughing. What makes me laugh is thinking of my mother and what she'd say to these bishops and cardinals and anyone else who was getting in the way of my relationship to Catholicism. I imagine my mother's big, pillowy Italian Catholic body, her soft, Italian-lady bosoms, her jiggly arms, her larger-than-life self with her enthusiastic, full-of-laughter-and-love-and-joy personality. I imagine her rising up, stretching out her arms, and standing between me and the Big C Church like she's about to break up a fight. I imagine my mother turning to that Big C disinviting Church and any other Catholic figures who have judged or failed to give me the benefit of the doubt, and I imagine the joy and laughter in her eyes falling away, her gaze shifting.

My mother could be fierce. Especially when it came to me.

Then I imagine how she'd give that Big C Church a piece of her mind. How she'd waggle her finger and become big enough to stand between me and all the bad parts of this tradition and do her best to protect me and scold them for how they've behaved. I imagine how they'd cower in the face of such love and such belief.

"Shame on you," she'd say to them. "How dare you."

There are also many years I feel as though there's nothing redeemable in this faith my mother tried so hard to give to me. But then I realize this is the real tragedy—that I cannot allow this faith that sustained my mother until the day she died and that she wanted for me to be ruined by the religious figures who power it. That I must learn to separate out the good my mother saw in it and the Big C Church and the terrible that often comes with it.

And even though the waters of doubt rose up again that day after mass, I did manage to keep a few things safe for myself—those precious moments of my mother and my grandmother appearing to me there in church. I found that I didn't care if anyone else thought it was true or not or if it was just me wishful thinking. What matters is that I felt it. It was real to me. So when I walk into a church now and sit down in the pew and close my eyes and let the presence of the people alongside me in the pews seep inside my heart, this setting brings the people I love the most back to me again. And maybe this is enough to let this faith be mine.

Part V
Writing toward God

24

I hear voices.

I am on my honeymoon. My husband is still asleep (the first one, the one who'll leave). Life is good, except for the part where he and I are staying in an open-air hut in Mexico, which is beautiful during the day but terrifying at night. Enormous bugs take flight in the darkness, animals scurry and scratch. Each time we go to bed, I am certain we'll be eaten by dawn. So far we survive, and overall, I am blissful. The sun is bright and hot as I swing in a hammock on our deck, which I discover is one of my favorite activities ever. I've never hung out in a hammock before my honeymoon. I vow to somehow string one up in the apartment in Burlington, Vermont, where we'll move after we're back. The ocean sparkles, the beach is glorious, and I am reading a novel that is making me laugh.

A young girl begins speaking to me as I lie there, swinging happily. Her voice is loud and clear, the sound of it unmistakable, and true. She tells me about her family, her teenage troubles, the fig trees in the yard behind her house, how she must bury them in winter so the trees survive the cold. *My name is Antonia Lucia Labella*, she says, *I live above my family's Italian market.* The voice isn't real, it's in my head. This girl is in my head.

I sip my coffee and stare out at the sea, listening to Antonia's laughter. Eventually my husband gets up from bed, we start our day and go down to breakfast. Antonia grows quiet.

Over the next few months, she continues to pop up, speaking in my head, rattling on about life, school, boys, and always those fig trees, always the Catholic saints, with whom she engages in a constant conversation. She knows about all of them, even the most obscure ones. Each time, her voice grows more familiar, more insistent, her story taking shape in my brain. I feel an urge to sit down and type out her words, capture her voice like I might take dictation, but I resist. I try to ignore her, to laugh her off. I don't do anything about her, not yet. I'm an academic, not a writer.

Within a year of getting married, my mother is gone. I am falling apart, my father is falling apart, my marriage is already crumbling under the weight of so much grief, too early in our married lives. I don't know how to be in the world without my mother in it. I am stumbling along trying to go to work and teach my students, trying to be a wife, trying to be a person, wondering how people do this—lose a parent, lose anyone, and continue in their ordinary lives. My heart is so heavy, I can barely drag myself places. My students see this, my colleagues see this, my husband sees this. My students are forgiving, my colleagues are not.

Antonia starts speaking again, she won't go away, and little by little I perk up. When I finally sit down to write her story, I don't think much about what will happen afterward. I just wake up and listen for the sound of her voice to appear in my mind. When it does, I follow it. I begin to look forward to the moments when she is speaking and I am listening, writing out all she says. She makes me laugh, and I need a reason to laugh. This laughter becomes like a rope dropped down into the darkness where I am living. I grab on to it, as Antonia's words whisper through me. I begin to recognize the voice, I recognize *her*, and then I know: Antonia's voice is my mother's voice as a girl, sprung forth from her stories about growing up in the Italian immigrant household of her childhood. Antonia has my mother's energy, her sense of humor, and most of all, her love for the saints.

I stop worrying if I am supposed to be following Antonia's voice as she tells me her story, I just let myself do it. Soon I am writing constantly, I am conjuring Antonia's entire world on the page each day, every chance I get. Doing so is the only thing that makes me smile during this time after my mother's death. I let myself have this small joy amid the pain and loss. I write to hear my mother's voice and imagine her alive and well and entertaining us with her energy and big ideas and constant stream of conversation with this saint and that other one. I write to conjure my mother. Antonia has arrived in the nick of time, she has come for me when I need her most.

Each time Antonia reaches out her hand, I learn to take it. I let her pull me along, lead me up and out of the abyss, Antonia and her friends and her family. My mother has let down this rope to me, still throwing me that lifeline even after her death. She dangles it in front of me until she and Antonia both are pulling with all their might. Soon we are our own parade, seeking the light.

"Writing is the only thing that makes me feel good," I tell my husband one day in the car. Nothing is going well for me in this moment.

He and I are struggling because I am so sad about my mother. Our house is a mess and I plead with him to help me keep it clean, but he doesn't, so the mess piles up. My father is not okay and I worry for his life, his grief is so total. Things at my professor job are a disaster and only grow worse after my mother dies. My departmental colleagues expect me to pretend like I am fine, and when I can't pretend, they reprimand me for all kinds of things, my clothing, my shoes, the fact that I shut my office door because I'm crying. They heap more and more work on me even though I can barely handle the work I already have. On top of this, I am showing symptoms of PTSD from what happened in graduate school and soon they are nearly constant. I feel like I am going crazy. Because, I kind of am. Everything is falling apart. I am falling apart.

All but when I am doing this one thing, this folly of mine, which is writing a novel.

In graduate school, my growing obsession with the medieval women mystics, with Hildegard of Bingen, Teresa of Ávila, Julian of Norwich, led me to make them the subject of my dissertation. I became fascinated with their relationship to God, how they spoke to God like God was a dear friend, even a spouse. They wrote of meeting God, of hearing God, a life with God, doing so with the passion and fervor and vividness of a novel, creating elaborate metaphors to share their visions of God, to try and teach their fellow nuns how to understand God and what God wants from us.

I both loved and was also maddened by those medieval women. I found their piety unbelievably frustrating, and occasionally annoying, because it was hard for me to relate to it. I wasn't blessed with that kind of piety. But I admired their conviction, the audacity of their visions and claims to know God and to have a direct experience of God, how this turned their faith into something solid and real. I learned to love how their claims brought them a special kind of religious authority unusual for women, and how they lived their lives in light of it, how they rose to direct entire communities of believers, how their stories inspired generations after them.

Not long after my first novel was bought and published, I was invited to give a talk at a festival of faith and writing. I titled my talk "I Hear Voices." I told everyone about the irony of how my writing comes to me, given my area of study in graduate school, those women mystics I fell in love with who also heard voices, but of a different sort. Or maybe not?

"I hear voices, too," I confessed to the people in the audience. I laughed while I said it, I laughed nervously the whole time. Like the situation of my writing was an oddly timed joke.

Meanwhile, I began to listen for other voices. I wondered who I might hear next.

I became a writer considerably late in life. Though I was always a reader.

Some of my favorite memories involve my mother packing us into the car so we could go off to the local library. We would sit in the children's section and look at books together for hours. When I got older, my mother let me go off into the stacks for children and spend ages picking out whatever I wanted. She would sit there patiently, waiting for me to make my decisions. She would laugh when I came out with a tower of novels, pushing the limits of how many books the library allowed a person to check out at once. We did this every week until I was old enough to go alone.

So much of who I am comes back to my mother. Even this part of me that has become a writer. Maybe especially this part. But while my mother was still alive, I didn't know that writing was ahead of me. After her death, I worried that the person she knew as her daughter was becoming altogether different, that she wouldn't recognize the woman I am today.

"Your mother knows."

My father always said this to me, whenever I raised this concern. He was so certain she was looking down upon us, witnessing the twists and turns of our lives after she was no longer in them. That she was watching from heaven as my life changed bit by bit, then drastically after my husband left and after my career as a professor didn't work out. My father was convinced she was still there supporting and protecting me every step of the way.

I worried she'd disapprove of the turns my life had taken, that she'd be angry, disappointed, even ashamed after I'd gotten divorced. When I admitted this to my dad, his convictions about my mother grew more fervent.

"No, Donna," he said. "Your mother knows, and she loves you and she is proud of who you are."

25

I write my way up and out of the abyss.

Ionce told one of my graduate professors that the only way to truly do philosophy is in a novel. That novels are the only place left where a person's ideas and questions are free to roam.

At the time, I was frustrated about the format academia required of our writing, the way it had to bump along, footnote to footnote, tethering every sentence with proof that you knew some-one else had already claimed the thought you were espousing. You were—are—only allowed to posit something slightly creative and of your own mind in basically the last paragraph of the paper, maybe the last full page if you're lucky. I thought this was ridiculous, mad-dening, unbelievably restrictive. I thought, what a way to kill any ideas a person might have.

Academic writing, scholarship, is a bit like poor Gulliver. You take these ideas of yours, big and exciting and hopeful, your brain full of plans, full of desire, and allow them to be laid right down on the ground, while these little worker bees get busy pinning them to the earth with ropes and knots and stakes. Until that desire of yours, all those theories spinning in your mind, cannot move, they lose their urgency, their momentum, you give them up, at least in their vibrancy. The good academic learns to do this herself, to tie down her own thoughts and ideas until they are empty of life, until they are barely anything more than an homage to what everyone else has already said. Until they are practically dead.

I believe in citing sources—of course I do. I have always loved the notion that when citing sources, we are acknowledging that our writing takes place in the context of a larger conversation, a kind of wonderful dinner party that calls upon the ghosts of other writers to join us in discussion. But at any good dinner party, the host is also allowed to speak, she is allowed to be heard. In the current version of academic writing, at least in my field, it requires her to be nearly silent, obedient, almost invisible, saying virtually nothing of merit. It ties her tongue much like the NDA I signed in graduate school, forbids her from taking risks with a pen. It makes her boring, steals her voice, douses the fire of her ideas. Expects them to be meek. Academia teaches you a lesson—the lesson being that you have nothing of real value to say. You are mainly meant to prove to others that you are widely read, to show the audience you know all the related material. The audience is like a tall wall, looming over you, blocking you, fencing you in. So to me it has always felt like staying still, treading water. You don't go anywhere. You get stuck in the cycle of proving, your fellow academics looking over your shoulder and sneering, or perhaps nodding, or shaking their heads in dismay.

The writing I've always admired, the philosophy and theology, the works of the mystics, spiritual figures medieval and contemporary, is of a different sort than what is expected of a scholar. It doesn't tie itself down so that it can't move, so that it moves nothing, not the heart or the soul or the mind, virtually powerless in the ways I believe count the most.

I want to be moved. I also want to *move*. Creative writing allows for movement. From one idea to the next, from one place to another. It is nimble. It allows the mind space to stretch out, the brain room to expand and breathe freely. It's also about relationship. In its movement, it moves from me to you, from you to me, connecting us. It establishes relationships, with characters who talk to you, the material you write, and also the audience who will eventually read it. Novels, memoirs, are invitations to be in relationship. They are a call out to the beyond.

I want my words to matter, to be that call out to the beyond that I cannot see, to move the heart and soul and mind—my own, and those of others. I want the freedom to say something that isn't already dead when it's left my mouth or is typed onto the page before me. I want writing to communicate, I want writing to take risks, to be vulnerable, to reveal something once hidden. I want to explore all of my questions without constraints. I've wanted my writing to allow me to search, to explore, to experiment. To solve mysteries.

I know this is a lot of desire, a lot of wants, but isn't desire at the heart of everything? Isn't desire at the heart of faith and what faith is? All those mystics and spiritual figures I fell in love with were nothing if not full of desire for God. Their writing is brimming with it, overflowing, and it spilled over onto me. I have it right now, I can see it brimming in my palms.

The more I write, the more I can see how writing is its own act of revelation. What we reveal depends on what we are writing at the time, but it's in the revelation that we may be moved, that readers may be moved, that those invisible connections and possibilities and meanings begin to weave themselves together to create something meaningful—where, through writing and reading, we find that we are not alone.

When I say all of this, I realize writing sounds a lot like a leap of faith. And I think that ultimately, I want my writing to be between me and God.

Hildegard of Bingen wrote of greenness. Greenness of spirit versus dryness of spirit.

There can be a greenness or dryness in creative writing. The call of the "literary" can turn writing dry. You try to adopt a certain lofty tone, you kill the heart in your writing for the sake of pretty sentences. You decide you are above all the ugly grit of human emotion, the longing, the messiness. Of plot. Of story. Of the things that call to our hearts. Of doubt, of things like faith and God. You revise the life out of your words. You excise the heart in favor of the critic, what the critic will say, the critic with the sneer on their face as they read, if that text still has its heart on its sleeve, if it's laid out right on the surface of the pages of a book, so vulnerable.

Hildegard was also a medical doctor during her lifetime, a healer who helped the women in her convent with things as ordinary as menstrual cramps; she was fascinated by plants and flowers, and especially the tender green insides of a stem. A sign of life and vibrancy, so also a sign of God. Something dry and dead, dusty, cracking, empty of water is akin to God's absence, the loss of the life force propelling all things. For Hildegard, our very souls can be green and they can also be dry, and spiritual dryness is akin to the Dark Night of the Soul.

The act of writing can be spiritually green, like cracking open the long, tender stem of a flower, the stalk of it brimming with water, with life, with a vibrancy that would have delighted Hildegard. Writing can open us when we do it, if we allow it, open our spirits, airing them out or allowing the spirit inside us to seep onto the page, like aloe, healing and soothing, a balm.

My dissertation director is the person who taught me to write books. That must sound ironic, given all I've said about my graduate program and about academic writing, and to anyone who's ever written a dissertation. Dissertations are known to be such miserable things, and yet mine was joyful.

Dr. Happel had bright-blue eyes that danced with humor, he was always throwing back his head and laughing. He was also a priest and always dressed as one, in the familiar black shirt and pants, white collar around his neck. As a monsignor, he also was a figure in the Big C Church, a man who worked at the university that harmed and silenced me. Yet he did all he could to help when others were doing all they could do to hinder. He risked himself and his position for me. He also swooped in to direct my dissertation because I would not have this other person do it. He would empower me in ways I'd need to survive in the future that I couldn't yet see but was coming.

He was a tall man, all willowy limbs, a lifelong runner. In fact, this is how he would die barely a few months after I graduated, during a run. This was only a few months before my mother would die as well, the same year I lost my grandma, all three of these important people in my life. But among the many gifts Dr. Happel offered were the following gems:

> *Your dissertation is not your life's work so don't make it so.*

> *Don't make any book your life's work—it's only just one book and there will be others.*

> *Forward, forward, forward—always move forward until you get to the end.*

Never revise until after you have a full draft because you can revise forever.

Write every day, even if you're having a bad writing day, because you can always revise.

A first draft shouldn't take longer than six months.

Because of Dr. Happel, I finished my dissertation in six months. His rules for writing dissertations and writing in general would seep into me and I'd keep to them for the rest of my life, all the way into the writing of novels and memoirs and every other thing I'd ever do on the page. Dr. Happel's voice, his encouragement, his theories for getting books done are woven into every book I've written. I can hear his voice now as I write these words.

But Dr. Happel also freed me from the burdens and restrictions of academic writing.

"You will write many different things over the course of your lifetime, Donna," he told me one day. We were sitting in his very grand office, him in a comfortable chair, me on the couch nearby, a coffee table between us, the light filtering through the tall stained glass windows on the other side of the room, arched and full of color. "Don't spend the rest of your life trying to publish your dissertation," he told me. "Your dissertation is a means to an end. After it serves its end, let it go. Don't let it trap you. Let yourself be *creative*. Let yourself say the things that *matter*. You could help to *change* things, do you know that?"

His voice that day, his words to me, rose from his body and up into the air, sparkling and loving and hopeful, and they settled over me like a fine dust. They settled into me and stayed, and when things in my career were at the darkest, I could feel them there, all that hope and faith he had in me. They would become one of the things that eventually save me. So many things would come to hurt me, but so many others would also come to save me.

So I was supposed to be writing boring academic articles during this time when my grandma, mother, and Dr. Happel died, in order to jump through the traditional academic hoops that professors must pass through on the road to tenure. But I was not doing it. I kept writing what I was not meant to write. Novels, opinion pieces, non-fiction books my colleagues refused to count as academically legitimate. I *had* to write them.

Much like faith, this felt like life or death.

Writing was saving me, and I needed saving. It became the thing I hung on to, that I did every day without fail. A lifeboat into which I'd climb and float across the wide, dark sea of grief, of the losses as they piled up. That tiny boat held together in the storm that was my life. Tossed and thrown and battered, it endured no matter what weather was upon me. I began to see writing as light.

All those years at Georgetown and in graduate school, I was searching for a way out of the darkness, trying to see beyond it to a something and not a nothing. Now, here I was and writing was becoming something. Something more than just words. I was building something real beyond the stories and the books themselves. Something I believed in; building my own boat across the darkness, the arms that would reach for me and pick me up. I was creating those arms, directing them to carry me. Or was I? Was it me or something more? Something else?

Isn't this what people have always done? Put pen to paper and hoped that through words they might find a way through, the way out—of grief, loss, of death and despair? The way toward *something more*? Isn't there a long tradition of people who've struggled with their own doubts, their agonies, their own existential despair by writing? People who write toward God? That even if it feels like I'm alone in this abyss when I plummet, I'm not alone at all? That I've never been alone down there? I've just needed to learn to see, to listen to the voices all around me that have been whispering this whole time? That in writing I am both saving myself and I am being saved?

I am being saved. But by whom?

26
My secret hope.

"Everything I write is about my mother," I told my husband one
night.

Not the first husband, the one who broke my heart, and not the
marriage that ended with me sobbing on the floor of the apartment
he and I once shared. This is a different husband, the second one.
Sometimes I can't believe I became someone who can talk about
having had a first and a second husband. I'm not here to talk about
them, though.

So I was telling Husband No. 2 that I could dedicate practically
everything I've written to my mother, because practically everything
I've written is about her in some way, shape, or form.

He wanted clarification. "What do you mean, everything is about
your mother?"

We were sitting at the long marble table with the wooden legs in our Brooklyn apartment. It's the same one I shared with the first husband. At night, for dinnertime, we like to turn on certain lights around the room to give the place a moody glow, with darkness at the edges of it all. A certain amount of darkness makes for good conversation, where you feel all right baring your soul if you need to. Maybe also a candle on the table, too, and of course, wine. Wine is also good for confessing and conversation, and Catholics do love their wine.

"It's like, when I write, I'm talking to my mother," I tell him. "I feel like I'm having conversations with her. And sometimes when I write, I can tell my mother something."

All of this is happening in Spanish, because No. 2 and I speak Spanish at home. But I'm nice so I'm translating for you.

My husband laughed. "So you're haunted by your mother."

I laughed, too, because it did sound like this was what I meant. "No, not haunted."

My mother has been gone twenty years as I write this. Her death seems far off in the distance. But for a long time after my dad and I lost her, I could barely speak about her, her death a looming shadow over her person, cloaking her in darkness. I would choke up with tears if I tried, or a pit of dread would open in my stomach.

I remember the moment I started coming out of this part of grieving her, because it coincided with a dream. I rarely dream about members of my family, or at least not dreams I can recall. Early on if I dreamt about my mother, it was usually horrific, because her death was pretty horrific. My dad and I were forced to witness my mother become someone else, become a nearly lifeless, wasting-away body.

In the dream I was in a Target in Manhattan. I'm pretty sure this was before they built an actual Target in Manhattan. But given how my mother did love to wander Target and Walmart and fantasized about being a greeter there, it seems fitting that this dream took place in Target.

The entrance of my dream-Target is right near Central Park, and I'm standing there, waiting for someone, I don't know who. Then in walks my mother, but not only her! In walks my grandma, too. They're wearing huge grins on their faces, my grandma with her short curly dyed blond hair and her reading glasses hanging from a chain like always. The three of us say hello like we've been hanging out every day of our lives, *Nope, nothing to see here.* They get a shopping cart, and I remember thinking, *Oh, so we're going to do this! We're going on a spree!* We wander all the aisles, Grandma's the one pushing the cart because she loved being in control of the shopping cart. The lights are bright overhead like they always are in Target, the shelves full, and we are just filling up our cart, laughing and talking and buying whatever we want.

Then I woke up.

I was so happy. I'd gotten to hang out with the two most important women in my life whom I hadn't seen in years and do so for a Target shopping spree. What could be better and more fun? Especially given that Grandma never turned down an opportunity to wander the aisles of a store where she could buy cheap nail polish and also flip-flops and also candy and also maybe a winter scarf. The dream seemed perfect. A special gift. Grace.

After the Target dream, the shadow of grief and loss blocking my mother moved. I could see her again in the light, Grandma, too. I could see them as they were alive, not only as they were while they were sick and dying. I could finally remember the happy times, the silly ones, the delicious ones, the boring ones. The angry ones, the fights that my mother and I had, the ways we tormented each other while I was a teenager. I was able to look back on all of it and take it in, a whole life I lived with this woman who wanted me so badly she spent twelve years waiting for me, and when I finally arrived, spent the rest of her time on this earth loving me in the way only a mother can.

Now that I've been a writer for many years, I can see that when I'm writing, I'm calling on my mother's wild imagination; that she gave me this part of myself, that I am using this part when I write, calling her through me and out of me and onto the page with all the words. Calling her back to me.

So that night with my husband and the food and the wine between us, candles flickering, I looked at him and said, "It's more like, when I write, I feel like I'm conjuring the dead."

I have told almost no one about this book. I only recently told Husband No. 2. His eyebrows arched when I mentioned that the subject of this memoir was faith. Then I took the conversation in a different direction.

Most people around me assume I am done with all of this faith business. That I left it behind long ago. The majority of the people in my life are horrified by religion, Christianity especially, Catholicism most especially. But a person can be horrified by what certain churches and traditions do, and still long for God in their hearts. A religion and its earthly trappings are not one and the same as the soul within us. Doesn't this whole faith business, this whole God business, have to be greater than even the Biggest Big C Church of all? Isn't that why I am—why any of us are—still here struggling to figure out our faith, if indeed we are?

My secret hope is that I will write my way through these trappings to something like faith, that this is what I am doing right now. That I am following in the footsteps of the likes of Teresa of Ávila, who traipsed room by room through the diamond caverns of her heart, sword in hand, in her fight to find God at the deepest center of herself. She fought and battled to push out all the noise around her, to reach the castle that is her soul, in order to better hear God's voice.

I am doing my best to better hear God's voice. Sometimes when I listen for the voices of my protagonists, I wonder whether one of them might be God. Or maybe if all of them are God.

While a big part of me is still full of doubt, a different part, one that gets bigger and stronger with time, doesn't care whether this is all just wishful thinking, because I am grateful to have been given such a gift. And whereas when my mother prayed for me and I accused her of taking my hard-earned achievements and owing them to God, the idea that God might be reaching for me through the words that flow through me like tiny, flickering lights, consoles me now instead of angering me. I no longer feel the need to be the sole owner of all I do. In fact, I'd prefer not to be.

But how does one take that very last step, the one that sends them off the diving board of faith? I am right there, and yet there is where I hesitate. The thought that maybe God and I are working together somehow gives me hope that maybe one day I'll find the courage to take that leap my mother tried to train me for while she was still alive.

I think writing is a miracle.

I often say these words to my students and friends and the writers I help with their books. I tell people that if they want to write, they should be willing to give everything over to the task; all that they are, without reservation. That if they are going to do this writing thing, they've got to be willing to *do* this writing thing. That this is how writing becomes a miracle. It's certainly how it's become my miracle. Sometimes, even, an act of resurrection.

I have faith in the power of writing.

I have faith in writing like my mother had faith in God.

There is a kind of proof, I suppose, in writing. I can rebuild the childhood home where I grew up. I can paint a portrait of its wine-red shutters, its cherry tree out front, its rooms filled with family living among porcelain saints kept under glass. Ironing boards, old television sets, favorite stuffed animals, and big children's Bibles open on my father's lap. I can conjure my mother and my grandmother, pull their voices from the past into the present, share their wisdom, remember it, honor it. Through writing I can have the conversations with my mother and now my father that we did not get to have while they were alive.

I have no trouble believing in what writing can do, I've felt its power flow through me, working to heal all it touches inside me, stitching my wounds closed with words. I let it bring me to my knees because I have faith it will pull me up and out of the darkness again, make me stronger, help me to stand and to walk again, eat and drink and be merry and laugh again. My writing is an unseen force that swirls in the air and I wait for it, to pull it down and make it visible on the page.

In my writing, I will toss myself from the highest diving board in the universe. In my writing, I am brave. I am as courageous as the greatest warrior. I will and do give of my whole self without holding back. I am most wholly myself. I am the best of me on the page. And when I'm at my worst, I restore myself through words. I type myself back to life.

Writing and words have become the arms that reach underneath me and pick me up and carry me across that terrible place where I can no longer walk on my own. Words have muscles and sinew and a body and legs and knees and feet and a torso that can bend and cradle and lift and move. When I am writing, my heart automatically opens, I am vulnerable by default, I trust and I trust naturally. I believe. I believe. *I believe.* I believe anything is possible—change, hope, new love, resurrection, Meaning. I have no resistance, my resistance falls away completely. I am wholly there, which is why it is also possible for me to heal through writing. I heal when I'm writing. I heal and I knit myself together and *I am knitted back together and I am healed.* It feels like me and it also feels like not me.

Maybe I simply need to let myself start there, stay there, be there in my writing.

Believe here. Leap from here.

Because what, really, is the difference between my faith in writing and faith in God? Is there any?

If writing is my creed, then this is my statement of beliefs: I do believe with my whole heart that my writing has saved me on multiple occasions. I believe it saves me still, that it will keep on saving me for the rest of my life. I even believe this very moment as I write the lines of this book, that my writing holds this potential and power. That it is somehow connected to something far beyond myself. That it is saving me right now, that this is its ongoing purpose in my life.

I know that my writing has reached down into the darkness where I have been lost and despairing on so many occasions in my life and has pulled me up out of the abyss and given me reason to hope again. I believe in the power of writing to conjure the dead, to allow me to have the conversations with those who are no longer with us by doing so on the page. I believe in the power of writing to heal us. To allow us to grieve. To remind us of awe and joy and laughter. Which is another way of saying, I suppose, that I believe in the Word.

Part VI
Wishful Thinking?

27

Portrait of love.

When my father died and I was going through the things he kept in his basement, I came upon a big cardboard box of photographs. One afternoon, I set about to go through them. In the mess of pictures from my father's childhood, my mother's childhood, pictures I will always cherish, I found a photograph I'd never seen before of my family.

It's of the three of us, my mother, my father, and me.

We are in Bermuda. I know the location because the photo is a formal portrait, an 8-by-10 print and it's nestled inside a large white card, with the name of the resort printed in shiny royal blue cursive lettering on the front. But the image itself isn't posed.

My parents are all dressed up, it looks like for a cocktail party, they have elegant crystal glasses in their hands, tulip in shape, the liquid is coral in color. My mother wears a long dress, with peach and green flowers on it, it cascades down her body. She's clearly been out in the sun, her skin is tan and glowing, her hair frosted in the way that women used to frost their hair. She looks so beautiful. My father is as tan as I've ever seen him, and his outfit makes me laugh. His tie is understated, navy blue, with a white, flower-like pattern, but with it he's wearing a bright-white dinner jacket, dark pants, and best of all, bright-white leather shoes. I'm pretty certain they have small wooden heels, you can just make them out in the back.

My parents make such a beautiful couple in this photograph. I love seeing them like this, gorgeous, fashionable, even glamorous. But the reason this photo has reached inside my heart ever since I pulled it from that long-forgotten box in my father's basement, is because there, standing between my parents, is me. I'm maybe four years old. Like my mother, I'm wearing a long dress, it's white and flowing with red trim, and it has a large curving red pocket on the front.

My parents are both looking down at me, below them.

They look so happy to have me with them, so pleased that I exist.

But what cracks me up is this:

I am looking straight into the lens of the camera. And I am glaring. I look like I'm about to throw a temper tantrum. It's so clear from the looks on my parents' faces that they know I am mad, that I am giving a death stare at the poor person behind that camera, that they find this unbelievably amusing. Like, they know me heart and soul, both the good and the bad, and they will love me despite this. They will keep me even with all my quirks and questions and resistance. Despite whatever tantrum is brewing inside me. Maybe even because of it?

As a writer, I have been disobedient, I have raged, I have thrown tantrums, I have loved and taken risks and shown my soul. I have displayed the ugliest things I have lived, the worst, the saddest, the most shameful. I have grieved and I have changed and I have also healed and laughed and hosted and lived wildly and imaginatively and loudly. I have found success and I have failed and I have tried my best. I have done all that I can. I have been the person that I am.

In my writing, I have been my parents' daughter, the one they are laughing about in that photo, the one they are loving despite even the hard parts. When I am writing, I imagine that I am calling their ghosts close, that my grandma joins them there, my mentor from graduate school, everyone I have loved and lost. I imagine them all dressed up and hovering over me, crystal wineglasses in hand, laughing, loving, holding me there, in that protective stance, their hands on my shoulders, making sure I am able to be myself, even when being me is difficult and painful and loud.

I want to believe. I want to be a person of faith. I want to be moved by God. I want there to be a heaven where my mother is sitting on some comfortable cloud, looking down at me with both judgment and love as I cook her recipes, as I do so by remembering the touch of her own hand as she once guided me at the stove and the cutting board. I want my parents to have reunited in death, I want them to be holding hands again, for eternity. I want my visits to the ocean, to the sea, to any body of water whatsoever, to be visits to my mother and my father. I don't want to be merely pretending this is the case because the ocean is where I spread both their ashes. I want it to be true. When once again I fall into the abyss because this is how I am made, I want to be rescued by God, by Jesus. I want to be able to sink into their arms, to let go and be carried across the darkness and into the light again. I want to stop trying to do all the hardest things on my own. As though there isn't also a God there with me in those depths and in all that isolation.

On the one hand, I am ashamed of myself for all of this. For so much wanting, so much wishing, so much need, especially when I am surrounded by friends and loved ones who don't share this same desire that is so potent in me, when the rest of the world seems to have moved on from religion and its corruptions and lies and whatever it might offer us. My desire for faith sometimes feels like this reality I wish I could hide from others.

But perhaps it is in this very same desire that my mother shows up in my genes, and how can I ever allow myself to be ashamed of that? That if my father gave me my darkness, then perhaps it is my mother who gives me this eternal restlessness as I wait for God and maybe will for the rest of my life. Maybe that is her gift to me, this want I can't shake to be a person of faith. Maybe the desire itself is the lifeline she was throwing me, and I've had it in my hands all along. Maybe if I just look down, there it will be, *right there*, bright and glowing and strong in my palms. Maybe I am the child of both my parents after all. And maybe that is just wishful thinking, but maybe it isn't. And maybe it doesn't matter either way if it is or it isn't or if you are ashamed of me or think I should be ashamed of myself or how you judge me for my words. After all, you are not God. None of us are.

When I look back now at that time in life when I chose my heart over academia, when I chose to write toward salvation rather than prove to my colleagues that I was worthy, when I wrote my way through the darkness of grief and loss and abuse and despair and rage and disappointment toward something like hope, toward connection and relationship instead of approval from the academic forces around me, I know I did the right thing. Even though doing so also brought grief and loss. But I wrote toward life, I chose to live, I chose to be in the mess of my humanity, in our humanity, in the way that only creative writing allows me to exist on the page. It was all that I could do anyway. There was no other way out but through, and through words.

My life as an adult has felt like a series of moments where things are okay and then they are not—they are *really* not. Whether it was the abuse, the tragedy of watching a parent struggle with cancer then die from that cancer, the shattering of certain dreams and trying to find others to replace them, the despair of losing a marriage and surviving a divorce, and then the death of a parent all over again, plus the regular challenges of life across it all, life seems to only get harder as I get older. I find myself wondering, how many wounds can a single person endure and still keep going?

The answer, I know, is all of them. That to be human is to be wounded again and again, to be wounded on top of our other woundings, to have life razed only to rebuild it and see it razed again. When once more I am standing atop the rubble, or trying to find my way out of it, I find myself dismayed that it's happened again. Life has happened again, my humanity has happened again. Most recently, when I lost my father, I finally faced the truth of it: that to be human is for life to happen again and again and again, in its beauty and in all of its tragic grief. That if there is any meaning to our humanity, this is *it*. To be human is to fall into the abyss and climb back out of it, only to fall and climb, fall and climb. I can choose to see myself as Sisyphus, choose to see life as a series of pointless successes and tragedies, or I can choose to see it as something else.

I can choose to see this cycle of woundings and subsequent survivals as signs that I am strong, that I am loved, that I endure, that maybe, maybe, despite all of this, I am not as alone as I once thought. Because even though I may feel alone and abandoned on so many occasions, I haven't actually been alone and abandoned—ever. That I may feel the darkness pressing in and it seems endless and unyielding, but it always eventually ends and yields, and the light shines in again. And while there are leaps of faith I still find so hard to take, there are others that seem as true and easy to me as the feet that carry me across the world and the cities within it.

It is also true that my parents loved me and they endure in my heart and in everything I see. That even when life has been at its worst, I have been deeply loved by the friends who are all around me. That even when I think I have nothing left inside me, that I cannot go on, there is always something left after all, and I do go on. Maybe somewhere within this cycle of the beauty and tragedy of our humanity, God has been reaching out to me through this raft of love I always manage to find in the darkness, whatever form it takes each time. There I am, hoisting myself up, *letting myself be hoisted up* so it can carry me out of the abyss and into the light again. That this is all that matters in the end, that the love somehow always reaches through the darkness to ferry me to safety, even if it takes years of paddling to arrive.

28

Last wishes.

The other day, I woke up after a vivid dream about my parents. In the dream, they were both alive, and I was young, maybe in college, or my early twenties. They were on their way to visit, and I was anxious, desperate to get everything around me under control before their arrival, attempting to wrangle my roommates into some semblance of organization as well as hide all the booze, kick out any of the boyfriends who stayed over, and basically get rid of all the evidence that might raise my mother's eyebrows and be a source of my parents' disapproval. My roommates were legion, there seemed to be twenty, even thirty, they were everywhere, and they were not interested in cooperating.

In the dream, I knew that my parents were getting closer and closer, that soon they'd arrive and everything would still be a mess. Even though they weren't there yet, I could also see them in the car, feel their presence like they were with me already, in the way that dreams allow many things to be true at the same time.

I became frantic, urging everyone around me to get going. "They're coming, hurry up!"

There came this moment in the dream when something terrible occurred to me. It hit me hard and fast and I immediately sensed the truth of it.

"Wait," I said to one of the roommates, whose face I could not make out clearly, "my father won't be here, because he is dead."

Even though my mother has been dead two decades longer than my father, it never occurred to me in the dream that she was also gone. I don't know why.

Then I woke up.

The dream startled me, it lingered, to experience my parents like this, as though they are still with me, as though they are still alive and I am still young and worried about what they'll think of me, or if I can measure up to their expectations. I've never dreamed about my parents like this, not together, and not from so many years ago in my life, close to when I was in college. The experience stole my breath, to realize how alive they seemed, as though they were never gone at all, not even for a day, or an hour. Even though in the dream I was worried and stressed and running around, trying to prepare for their arrival, I woke up grateful. It was as if, while asleep, I got to time-travel to hang out with them again. It was all so real.

The dream, a gift. Another grace.

Like they reached out from the beyond to tell me they're still with me.

To reassure me they're together now, just like when I was young.

As I work on this book, I have other dreams about my family, which makes sense because I am writing about them here. But also strange because, like I said, I don't normally dream about them, I don't normally have the privilege of seeing the people I've lost alive and well again when I'm asleep. Dreams can be terrible but they can also be wonderful gifts. I am not normally prone to those gifts. But lately the dead have been visiting me at night.

The dream I have this morning before I wake is about my grandmother. I haven't seen her in decades. Not in real life and not since my Target dream.

In the dream, my father has died, and my mother is long gone, and what is left is the task of packing up all the things in my father's house. But in the dream, my father still lives in the Rhode Island house where I grew up, not in the house where he lived long after we lost my mother. My childhood bedroom is still there, with all my childhood things, nearly untouched from when I was little. There I am, walking down the hallway, knowing that I am about to have to go through everything in my father's house so soon after losing him; that this is going to be so hard.

I head through the doorway of my room, and there is my grandmother!

"Hi, sweetheart," she says. She is taking apart something as she talks, maybe the legs of a table, like the kind you might get at IKEA. "You don't have to worry about this, I'll do it."

A wave of gratitude washes over me. "Okay, thanks, Grandma," I tell her, and turn around, go back down the hall, relieved because I was dreading this task. But then as I walk away, several things strike me in quick succession.

Where did my grandma come from, when did she arrive? I haven't seen her in so long! And wow, somehow my grandmother outlasted both of my parents, and here she is, the only person left still standing in my family aside from me. Isn't that so strange, that she survived both of them?

At this point, I am flooded with a realization that Grandma—who I haven't seen in years—is right here with me in the house! So I turn around, and race back into my childhood room, worried that maybe I'll get there and find her gone. But no, she's there, and I see her again, bright and alive and so very herself, with her permed and dyed blond hair, her short stature, her energetic movements, just going along working and humming as she does.

Grandma realizes I've returned, she looks up and smiles and says, "Sweetheart!"

In the dream, I go to her, there is a mixture of shock and gratitude that I am seeing her—in the dream, she is definitely alive but something in me also knows this is not quite true. I give her a great big hug, and it's *so real*. I can feel her in my arms, my hands on her back, my head on her shoulder. "Grandma," I tell her in the dream, "I know I haven't said this in a while, but you know I love you so much, right? I've always loved you so much, I *love* you, Grandma!"

I say it three times and I can feel her there, like her arms are around me now, and it is still all so real, like it is *happening*, and I feel so lucky that I've made sure to tell my grandma how much she means to me before I lose her, too. Like I've lost both my parents.

Then I wake up.

I know it was only a dream, that of course my grandmother didn't outlast either of my parents, that when she actually died, I wasn't there and didn't get to say goodbye. But the dream was just so real and I can still feel her in my arms and hear her voice like she's in the room with me right now, I can hear myself telling her I love her and know with my whole heart that she is hearing me and she knows it, too, that she's always known it, all these years she's been gone, she's still known it.

I feel like my grandmother did this on purpose, that she somehow came to me in the dream to let me know she's still there for me, with me, that even though both my parents are gone, she's been with me this whole time and wanted me to know this, and maybe just wanted to say hello, and give me one more hug. That she decided to pay me a visit, that she found the will and the power or she cashed in some chits and used everything she still is in the beyond and who she was in life in order to show up during the deepest dark moment of the night to say hello, to see her granddaughter, to spend some time with me as though she was never gone at all.

And maybe she never was.

Do I dare to let myself believe? Is it just wishful thinking to allow myself?

If I am honest, I think I will always have doubts, I will always struggle, I will always have Dark Nights of the Soul and long walks through the wilderness, that this is just part of who I am. It would be a lie to pretend that all is resolved, that I will never slide down into the abyss again, that I am suddenly now a person of faith. But this is not all I am, either, a person who doubts and falls, and while the abyss will always be a part of me, a place that will take me at times, it is not the only place I live. In fact, I mostly reside elsewhere, in the land of the living.

Isn't all of this just what it means to be alive? We fall, we rise, we fall again, we try, we fail, we try again, we are eclipsed by darkness sometimes and then, somehow, miraculously, we find the light, the light comes, it shines upon us, and it shows us the way through and there we are, on the other side again, at least for a time. A wonderful, glorious time.

When I look around my life, the actual physical, human nature of it, it is not a perfect life by any means. But it is a life full of love. I see love all over the place, strewn about, a happy, disorganized mess of it. In my parents' wake, in my grandma's wake, they left a bubbling trail of love in which I can swim and laugh and even water-ski, their love as big as the sky and the seas, so vast that I cannot fail to see it every single day of my life even though they're all gone. If that's not a miracle, then what is a miracle, really? If that isn't God, then what could God be?

Can I dare to let myself have this, once and for all, or even just for once in my life?

It feels so scary to think of saying I am a person of faith.

I've said that I'm not, that I can't be, for so very long.

But I have faith in all the words I've said here in this book.

Everything I've written.

And when I look back on it all, and reread what I've said, I can't help but see what's there. It's right in front of my face in black and white.

And it sure looks a lot like faith.

Acknowledgments

This was a difficult book to write. I've wanted to do this memoir for a long time, specifically with my wonderful editor, Beth Adams. Beth has known about my struggles with faith and doubt for as long as we've been friends. (We are getting up there, Beth, I feel like we're approaching two decades!) But we signed up the book, and then, very unexpectedly, my beloved father died. He is the person I'd spoken with every day since we lost my Mom, sometimes twice, for nearly twenty years. Afterward, I didn't know how I was going to get through each day, never mind write this book—especially *this* book, which was always going to be about my family.

But when he died, the people I love showed up in force to help me build my most recent lifeboat and to celebrate my father in Brooklyn when celebrating him in Rhode Island didn't work out. You know who you are, but I need to mention a few people in particular: Kylie and Lauren, who talked me all the way through my Long Dark Night of driving to the hospital to say good-bye to my dad. Marie, who rushed to my apartment in Brooklyn when I got back, bringing with her a giant bag of sustenance from Eve. Alvina and Stephen, who showed up to handle the flood in my apartment, and Denise and

Vinny, who invited me to stay while my apartment was getting fixed and showed me so much hospitality, love, and kindness. Sarah, who went with me to see the sequel to *Top Gun* on a particularly difficult day of grieving. I will never forget these above-and-beyond acts of love and generosity.

Maybe it's strange to thank the people who showed up for me after my father died, but without all that love, I couldn't have opened my laptop to start writing again. So, thank you for helping me to put the pieces of my life and heart together again. Without you and all you did, this book wouldn't exist.

On the note of this book, I want to thank Beth Adams from the bottom of my heart for fighting for this memoir to exist, for believing in me and the writing, and for having faith that I could—and should—tell this story. I am grateful, too, for all the extensions when things didn't turn out as we planned. I also want to thank all of Beth's colleagues at Hachette Nashville for being excited to publish a memoir about someone filled with doubt, because you believe that I am not alone and that we need stories about the difficulties of being a believer. Thank you for your faith.

Rene and Carlene, thank you for the many years of conversation about faith, spirituality, religion, Catholicism, the mystics and saints, Dorothy Day and God and Jesus, and the centrality of these things in our lives, as well as the importance of having the space to write about them. To Amy Scher, for showing up in my life like one of my mother's angels right after I lost my dad and making me laugh nearly constantly. To Miriam, as always, for your many decades of support as my agent and also as my friend and for all the food we ate in Barcelona while I was writing this. And of course, to Daniel (Husband #2), for being there in all the ways you have, especially during this very difficult year of sadness and my attempts to write through it. I am grateful for you and for our life in Barcelona—the city that has been such a huge part of my healing.

Lastly, to my parents, Concetta and Raymond, for loving me so unconditionally and truly that I still feel your love every day. Without you both, I wouldn't have become a writer and then I wouldn't have found the means to work through the grief of living and the pain of loss or the courage to write toward joy and hope, despite it all, and most especially for teaching me that it's okay, even totally normal, to talk to the dead.

About the Author

Donna Freitas has written more than twenty books, both fiction and nonfiction, for adults, children, and young adults. Among them are *Consent: A Memoir of Unwanted Attention* (Little, Brown), *Sex and the Soul: Juggling Sexuality, Spirituality, Romance, and Religion on America's College Campuses* (Oxford University Press), and *The Nine Lives of Rose Napolitano* (Viking/Penguin), which has been translated into twenty languages. She has written for the *Washington Post*, the *New York Times*, and the *Wall Street Journal* and has appeared on radio and television from NPR's *All Things Considered* to CNN and the *Today* show. Donna loves cooking, spending time with her friends, and eating. She and her husband split their time between Barcelona and Brooklyn.